The Epistles of
I, II, III John

... And the common people heard him gladly. Mark 12:37

Common People Series
Paula Land

THE PURPOSE OF THIS GUIDE

*Mark 12:37...**And the common people heard him gladly***

The twelfth chapter of Mark begins with Jesus teaching a parable and as usual, the Pharisees, Sadducees and scribes began to flaunt their scholarly knowledge and tried to snare Him in His own words. In the background, is another group of people known as the common people.

.... And the common people heard him gladly.

As in Biblical times, common people are not less intelligent but many do lack confidence and encouragement to read the Word of God. The lack of confidence in our ability to read and learn the scriptures discourages us from actually reading them. What seems as a lack of confidence in ourselves, however, is wrongly placed false humility. It is our lack of FAITH in the Holy Spirit to teach us to skillfully handle the Word of God.

This study guide includes both general Bible knowledge and deeper studies. But it's intent is not just to impart knowledge. Ultimately, it is to help you increase your faith in the Holy Spirit that **He will guide** and teach **you** to skillfully handle the Word of God. You may at first follow this guide to the letter. But it won't be long before you are allowing the Holy Spirit to lead you through your own reading.

*John 16:13 **Howbeit when he, the Spirit of truth, is come, he will guide you into all truth: for he shall not speak of himself; but whatsoever he shall hear, that shall he speak.***

The Bible is the inspired Word of God and consists of 66 books. You can follow this inspiration from one book of the Bible to the next by looking for shadows, patterns, similiarities and cross references. I have included my own studies to help you learn how to recognize some of these.

This guide will also be of great value to those who are searching the scriptures for the deeper things of God. *1 Corinthians 2:10 **But God hath revealed them unto us by his Spirit: for the Spirit searcheth all things, yea, the deep things of God.*** The format enables you to visualize small details that our brains may choose to skip because of information overload. It is invaluable in discerning the proper context of each passage while organizing people, places, dates and sequence of events.

HOW TO USE THIS GUIDE

1. **You must use the King James Bible.** All answers correspond to the King James Bible. There is no substitute.

2. The chapters are divided into sections. Each section has two pages. The lower page is titled NOTES. On this page you will discover words that you overlooked in your reading and write you own study notes. I have intentionally used pictures that are black and white, faceless, and unremarkable to avoid preconceived notions and ideas.

3. The opposite page (GUIDE) has the completed verses. Also written in *script* are my notes. Some of these notes are as simple as definitions of words or phrases that may be unfamiliar and possibly hinder the understanding. Others are deep Bible studies that leaves us in awe of God's Word.

4.   <u>This is very important</u>. Fill-in each blank in numerical order because they are numbered according to the sequence of events. Some pages contain a lot of information and are very busy. Each blank already has the first letter already completed so you don't lose your thoughts trying to figure out what is being asked.

(1)   (2)   (3)

5. <u>Don't try to study outside sources to clarify the meaning.</u> <u>There is no historical or archaeological information from antiquities or Greek/Hebrew lexicons included</u>. These aren't necessary because the King James Bible is plenary meaning complete. If you want to do a deeper study, search the Bible for similiar verses, phrases or ideas. You can find these easily using a concordance (a book that lists words of the Bible in alphabetical order). The Webster's 1828 Dictionary is an excellent source to find definitions to biblical words that may have dropped out of today's vocabulary.

6. Maps are used for general locations only. They are not exactly to scale and serve to keep places and events in context.

Read Chapter 1

Psalm 119:11 Thy word have I hid in mine heart, that I might not sin against thee.

John, the disciple who calls himself the one whom Jesus loved wrote both the Gospel According to John and The First Epistle of John.

John begins both books similarly

The Epistle of 1 John	Gospel of JOHN
V. 1 *That* which was from the *beginning*	**John 1:1 In the beginning was the Word,** That is referring to the Word, Jesus
V.1...which *we* have seen with our *eyes,* which we have looked upon, and our hands have *handled,* of the *Word* of life;	"we" is referring to John and the other disciples of Jesus. They actually saw him physically and not that their eyes were opened spiritually. They also physically touched him after the resurrection.
V.2 (For the *life* was *manifested,* manifest means to clearly visible	**John 1:14 And the Word was made flesh, and dwelt among us, ...**
V.2 and *we* have *seen* it →*John and other disciples*	**... (and we beheld his glory, the glory as of the only begotten of the Father,) full of grace and truth.**
V.2 ...and *bear witness,*	**John 15:27 And ye also shall bear witness, because ye have been with me from the beginning**
V.2 and shew unto you that *eternal life,*	**John 5:11 And this is the record, that God hath given to us eternal life, and this life is in his Son.**
V.2 which was *with the Father,*	**John 1:1 In the beginning was the Word, and the Word was with God**
V.2 and was *manifested* unto *us;)*	**John 17:6 I have manifested thy name unto the men which thou gavest me out of the world:**

CHAPTER 1 V.1-2

The Epistle of 1 John

Gospel of JOHN

The Epistle of 1 John	Gospel of JOHN
V. 1 *T*_____ which was from the *b*_____	**John 1:1 In the beginning was the Word,**
V.1...which *w*_____ have seen with our *e*_____, which we have looked upon, and our hands have *h*_____, of the *W*_____ of life;	
V.2 (For the *l*_____ was *m*_____,	**John 1:14 And the Word was made flesh, and dwelt among us, ...**
V.2 and *w*_____ have *s*_____ it	**... (and we beheld his glory, the glory as of the only begotten of the Father,) full of grace and truth.**
V.2 ...and *b*_____ *w*_____,	**John 15:27 And ye also shall bear witness, because ye have been with me from the beginning**
V.2 and shew unto you that *e*_____ *l*_____,	**John 5:11 And this is the record, that God hath given to us eternal life, and this life is in his Son.**
V. 2 which *w*_____ *t*_____ *F*_____,	**John 1:1 In the beginning was the Word, and the Word was with God**
V.2 and was *m*_____ unto *u*_____;)	**John 17:6 I have manifested thy name unto the men which thou gavest me out of the world:**

CHAPTER 1
V. 3-5
Key

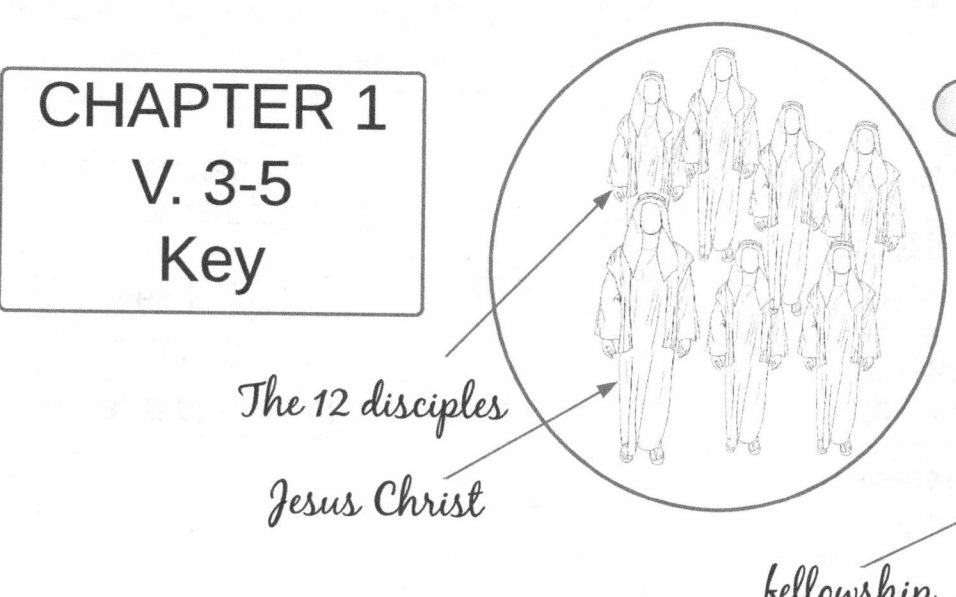

The 12 disciples

Jesus Christ

1

Disciples

V.3 That which we have seen and heard declare we unto you, that ye also may have *fellowship* with us: and truly *our fellowship* is with *the Father,* and with his *Son Jesus Christ.*

John 17:21 That they all may be one; as thou, Father, art in me, and I in thee, <u>that they also may be one in us</u>: that the world may believe that thou hast sent me.

fellowship

2 V.4 And these things *write we* unto you, that your *joy* may be full.
John 17:13

Knowledge of
Jesus

3 V.5 This then is *the message* which we have *heard of him*

V.5 *God is light, and in him is no darkness at all.*

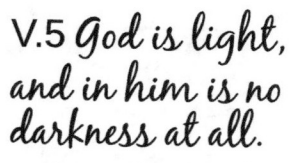
Heaven

But light is not God

Jesus

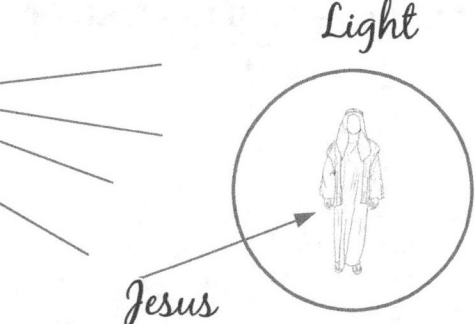
Light

Darkness

Absence of God

1

V.3 That which we have seen and heard declare we unto you, that ye also may have
f_____ with us: and truly o_____
f_____ is with t_____ F_____,
and with his S_____ J_____ C_____.

2 V.4 And these things w_____ w_____ unto you, that your
j_____ may be full. **John 17:13**

3 V.5 This then is *the* m_____ which we have h_____ of h_____

V.5 G_____ is
l_____, and
in h_____ is
n_____
d_____ at
a_____.

Heaven

Light

Darkness

Absence of God

John 1:9 That was the <u>true Light,</u> which lighteth every man that cometh into the world.

Walk in the light

Walk in the darkness

Heaven

Absence of God

John is writing to saved people on how to have fellowship with the Father and Son. If we do not confess the sin in our lives, that fellowship will be broken. Our salvation is not affected. It is eternal but our fellowship with Him will be lost.

saved

2 V.7 But if we *walk in the light,* as he is in the light, we have *fellowship* one with another, and the *blood of Jesus Christ his Son cleanseth us from all sin.*

1 V.6 If we say that we have *fellowship* with him, and *walk in darkness, we lie,* and do not the truth:

saved

4 V.9 If we *confess our sins,* he is faithful and just to forgive us our sins, and to *cleanse us from all unrighteousness.*

3 V.8 If we say that we have *no sin,* we deceive ourselves, and the *truth is not in us.*

5 V.10 If we say that *we have not sinned,* we make him *a liar,* and his *word is not in us.*

Sanctify means set apart.

John 17:17 Sanctify them <u>through thy truth: thy word is truth.</u>

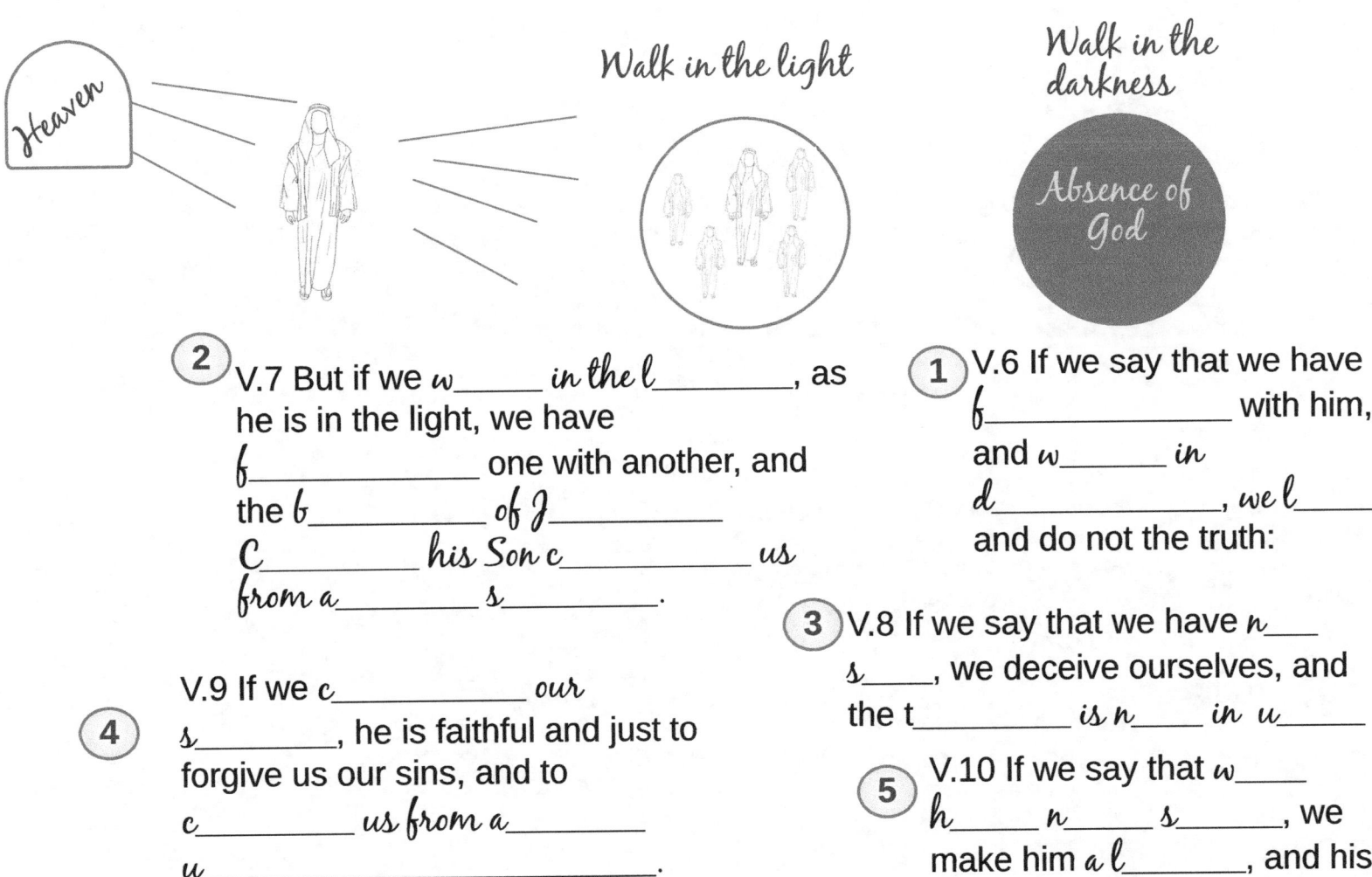

Heaven

Walk in the light

Walk in the darkness

Absence of God

2 V.7 But if we w_____ in the l_____, as he is in the light, we have b_____ one with another, and the b_____ of J_____ C_____ his Son c_____ us from a_____ s_____.

1 V.6 If we say that we have b_____ with him, and w_____ in d_____, we l_____, and do not the truth:

4 V.9 If we c_____ our s_____, he is faithful and just to forgive us our sins, and to c_____ us from a_____ u_____.

3 V.8 If we say that we have n____ s_____, we deceive ourselves, and the t_____ is n_____ in u_____

5 V.10 If we say that w_____ h_____ n_____ s_____, we make him a l_____, and his w_____ is n_____ in u____.

Read Chapter 2

Psalm 12:6 The words of the LORD are pure words: as silver tried in a furnace of earth, purified seven times.

John 21:15 So when they had dined, Jesus saith to Simon Peter, Simon, son of Jonas, lovest thou me more than these? He saith unto him, Yea, Lord; thou knowest that I love thee. He saith unto him, Feed my lambs.

1Peter 2:2 As newborn babes, desire the sincere milk of the word, that ye may grow thereby:

1 V.1 *My little children*, these things write I unto you, that *ye sin not*. And if any man sin, we have an *advocate* with the Father, *Jesus Christ the righteous:*

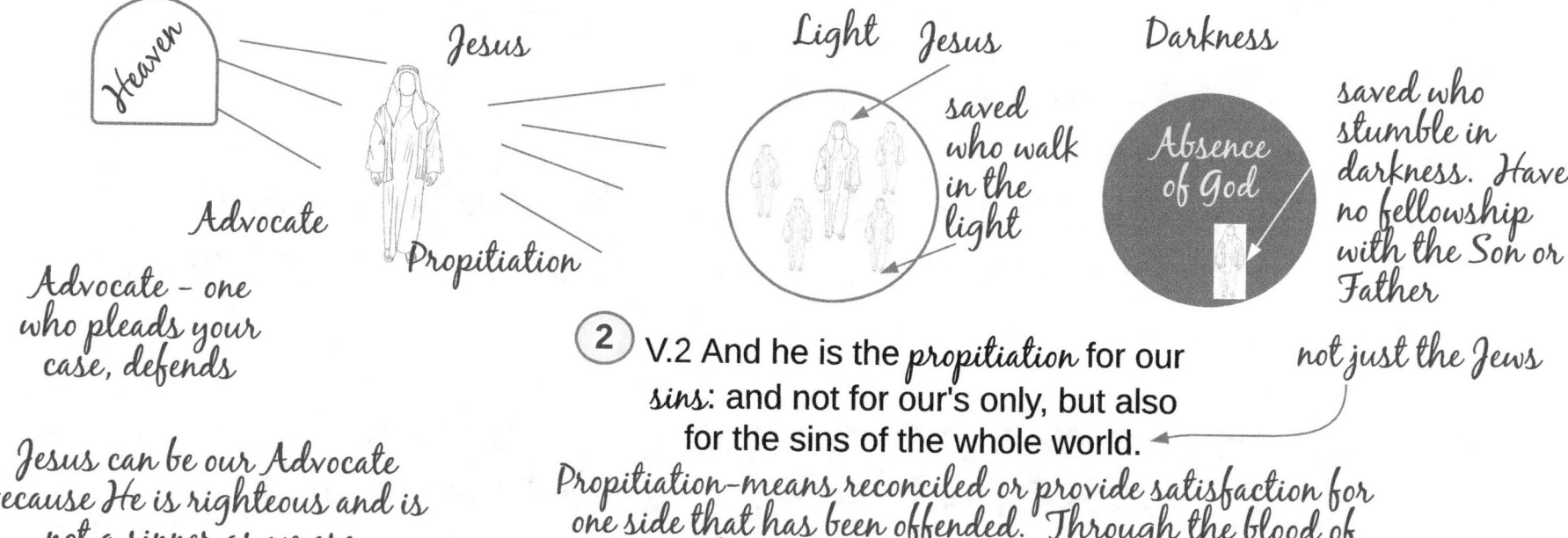

Heaven

Jesus

Advocate

Propitiation

Light   Jesus

saved who walk in the light

Darkness

Absence of God

saved who stumble in darkness. Have no fellowship with the Son or Father

Advocate – one who pleads your case, defends

Jesus can be our Advocate because He is righteous and is not a sinner as we are.

2 V.2 And he is the *propitiation* for our *sins*: and not for our's only, but also for the sins of the whole world.

not just the Jews

Propitiation—means reconciled or provide satisfaction for one side that has been offended. Through the blood of Jesus Christ we have been reconciled to the Father

John 1:29 The next day John seeth Jesus coming unto him, and saith, Behold the Lamb of God, which taketh away the sin of the world.

(1) V.1 M_____ l_____ c_____, these things write I
unto you, that y_____ s_____ n_____. And if any man sin, we have an
a_____ with the Father, J_____ C_____ the
r_____:

Heaven   Jesus   Light   Darkness

Absence
of God

(2) V.2 And he is the p_____
for our s_____: and not for our's
only, but also for the sins of the
whole world.

(1)

V.3 And *hereby*
we do know <u>that we know him,</u>
if we keep his commandments.

The 1st Epistle of John
tells us how <u>we may know</u>
many things.
Beginning with "How we
do know that we know
Him.

**1 John 4:9 In this was <u>manifested the love of God toward us,</u>
because that God sent his only begotten Son into the world,
that we might live through him.**

Heaven

Light

Darkness

*Love of God is
manifested*

Absence of
God

*fully
manifested* (2)

*guard or retain,
don't let escape*

**1 John 3:24 And he that <u>keepeth</u>
his commandments dwelleth in
him, and he in him...**

(3) V.5 But whoso *keepeth* his
word, in him verily is the
love of God *perfected*:
hereby *know we* that we are
in him.

V.4 He that saith, *I
know him*, and
keepeth not his
commandments, is
a liar, and the
truth is not in him.

abiding (dwelling in Him.)

(1) **V.3 And _____**
we do know that we know him,
if we keep his commandments.

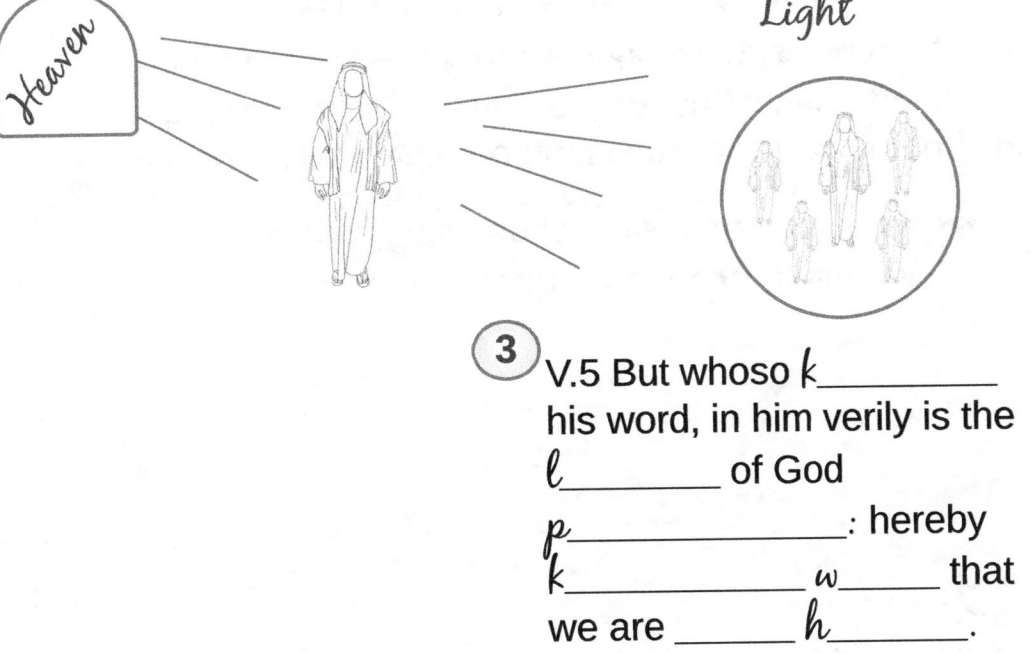

Light

Darkness

Absence of God

(3) V.5 But whoso k_____
his word, in him verily is the
l_____ of God
p_____: hereby
k_____ w_____ that
we are _____ h_____.

(2) V.4 He that saith,
I_____ k_____
h_____, and
k_____
n_____ his
commandments, is a
l_____, and the
t_____ is n_____
____ h_____.

CHAPTER 2
V.6-12
Key

7 V.12 I write unto you, *little children*, because your sins are forgiven you for his name's sake.

newborn babes–doctrine of salvation

John 4:8 He that loveth not knoweth not God; <u>for God is love.</u>

Light

Darkness

Heaven

Absence of God

saved

1 V.6 He that saith he *abideth* in him ought himself also so to walk, even as he *walked*.

2 V.7 *Brethren*, I write no new commandment unto you, but an old commandment which ye had from the beginning. The *old commandment is the word* which ye have heard *from the beginning*.

3 V.8 Again, a *new commandment* I write unto you, which thing is true in him and in you: because *the darkness is past*, and the *true light* now shineth.

5 V.10 He that *loveth* his *brother abideth* in the *light*, and there is *none* occasion of *stumbling* in him.

4 V.9 He that saith he is in the light, and *hateth* his *brother*, is in *darkness* even until now.

6 V.11 But he that *hateth* his *brother* is in *darkness*, and *walketh* in *darkness*, and knoweth not whither he goeth, because that *darkness* hath *blinded* his eyes.

Those who are saved but do not keep His commandments are blinded by the darkness and stumbles in life.

⑦ V.12 I write unto you, l_____ c_____, because your sins are forgiven you for his name's sake.

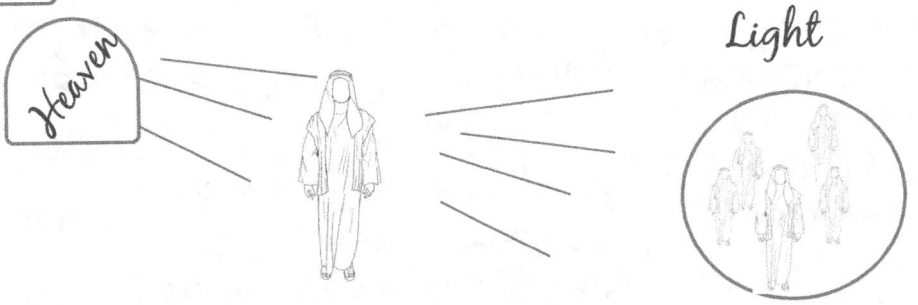

Heaven

Light

Darkness

Absence of God

① V.6 He that saith he a_____ in him ought himself also so to walk, even as he w_____.

② V.7 B_____, I write no new commandment unto you, but an old commandment which ye had from the beginning. The o_____ c_____ is the w_____ which ye have heard f_____ the _____.

③ V.8 Again, a n_____ c_____ I write unto you, which thing is true in him and in you: because the d_____ is p_____, and the t_____ l_____ now shineth.

⑤ V.10 He that l_____ his b_____ a_____ in the l_____, and there is n_____ occasion of s_____ in him.

④ V.9 He that saith he is in the light, and h_____ his b_____, is in d_____ even until now.

⑥ V.11 But he that h_____ his b_____ is in d_____, and w_____ in d_____, and knoweth not whither he goeth, because that d_____ hath b_____ his eyes.

John 21:15 ...Feed my lambs.
John 21:16...Feed my sheep.
John 21:17...Feed my sheep.

Jesus said this to Peter just before Peter was to begin his own ministry. These are stages of spiritual growth. He is to feed all the flock not just one group.

After the resurrection, Jesus called the disciples children. Now John is a father writing to others.

Fathers (Sheep)	Young Men (Sheep)	Little Children (Lambs)
V.13 I *write* unto you, *fathers*, because ye have known him that is from the beginning. *Write is present tense*	V. 13 I *write* unto you, *young* men, because ye have overcome the wicked one. *Write is present tense*	V. 3 I *write* unto you, little children, because ye have known the Father. *Has never written to them before because they are newborn babes*
V.14 I *have written* unto you, *fathers*, because ye have known him that is from the beginning. *(have written–in the past)*	V. 14 I *have written* unto you, *young men*, because ye are *strong*, and the word of God abideth in you, and ye have overcome the wicked one. *(have written– in the past)*	*Mature Christians need the meatier preaching on fleshly lusts. Carnal Christians are little children and need the milk of the word such as doctrine of salvation and love of God*

John wrote both books. (1) The Gospel According to John and (2) The First Epistle of John. The fathers and young men have read the Gospel According to John. Therefore, John says I have written to you. When he speaks to little children he does not say, I have written but only that I write referring to this book, The First Epistle of John. The majority of this book is addressed to little children with the milk of the word such as fellowship. Only a few verses addresses the fathers and young men which speaks of the lust of the flesh.

1Corinthians 3:1 And I, brethren, <u>could not speak</u> unto you as unto spiritual, but as unto <u>carnal</u>, even as unto <u>babes in Christ.</u>
<u>1Corinthians 3:2 I have fed you with milk, and not with meat:</u> for hitherto ye were not able to bear it, neither yet now are ye able.
For ye are yet <u>carnal</u>:

Apostle Paul preaching to the Corinthians because they were carnal and not growing.in Christ.

John 21:15 ...Feed my lambs.
John 21:16...Feed my sheep.
John 21:17...Feed my sheep.

Fathers (Sheep)	Young Men (Sheep)	Little Children (Lambs)
V.13 I w_____ unto you, f_____, because ye have known him that is from the beginning.	V. 13 I w_____ unto you, y_____ m_____, because ye have overcome the wicked one.	V. 3 I w_____ unto you, little children, because ye have known the Father
V.14 I h_____ _____ unto you, f_____, because ye have known him that is from the beginning.	V. 14 I h_____ w_____ unto you, y_____ m_____, because ye are strong, and the word of God abideth in you, and ye have overcome the wicked one.	**1Corinthians 3:1 And I, brethren, <u>could not speak</u> unto you as unto spiritual, but as unto carnal, even as unto <u>babes in Christ.</u> <u>1Corinthians 3:2 I have fed you with milk, and not with meat:</u> for hitherto ye were not able to bear it, neither yet now are ye able. For ye are yet <u>carnal</u>:**

CHAPTER 2
V.15-17
Key

John 2:14 <u>I have written unto you, fathers,</u> because ye have known him that is from the beginning. <u>I have written unto you, young men,</u> because ye are strong, and the <u>word of God abideth in you,</u> and ye have overcome the wicked one.

only verses in this book addressed to the fathers and young men.

The World

lust of the flesh, lust of the eyes, pride of life

passeth away

V.15 Love not the *world*, neither the *things* that are in the *world*. If any man love the world, the love of the Father is not in him.

V.16 For all that is *in the world*, the *lust of the flesh*, and the *lust of the eyes*, and the *pride of life*, is not of the Father, but is *of the world*.

3 fleshly sins (1) lust of the flesh (2) lust of the eyes (3) pride of life

lust of the flesh

Genesis 3:6 And when the woman saw that the tree was <u>good for food</u>, and that it was <u>pleasant to the eyes</u>, and a tree to be <u>desired to make one wise</u>, she took of the fruit thereof, and did eat, and gave also unto her husband with her; and he did eat.

lust of the eyes

pride of life

Satan tempted Jesus with these 3 sins

Matthew 4:3... command that these stones be made bread. *(lust of the flesh)*

Matthew 4:6...lest at any time thou dash thy foot against a stone. *(Pride of life)*

Matthew 4:8 ...sheweth him all the kingdoms of the world, and the glory of them; *(lust of the eyes)*

V.17 And the *world passeth away*, and *the lust* thereof: but he that doeth the *will of God abideth for ever.*

John 2:14 I have written unto you, fathers, because ye have known him that is from the beginning. I have written unto you, young men, because ye are strong, and the word of God abideth in you, and ye have overcome the wicked one.

V.15 Love not the w_____, neither the t_____ that are in the w_____. If any man love the world, the love of the Father is not in him.

V.16 For all that is _____ the w_____, the l_____ of the f_____, and the l_____ of the e_____, and the p_____ of l_____, is not of the Father, but is of the w_____.

V.17 And the w_____ p_____ away, and the l_____ thereof: but he that doeth the w_____ of g_____ a_____ for e_____.

The remainder of the First Epistle of John is written to Little Children

John 21:15 Feed my lambs

V.18 *Little children,*

...that there should be time no longer. Rev. 10:6

last period of time

that – refers to a certain antichrist. (Satan)

V.18 It is the *last* time: and as ye have heard *that* antichrist shall come,

even now are there *many* antichrists;
whereby *we know* <u>that it is the last time</u>.

antichrist is a general term meaning against Christ.

skeptical of deceivers but then saw miracles and prophecies

John 6:14 Then those men, when they had seen the miracle that Jesus did, said, This is of a truth <u>that</u> prophet that should come into the world.

Jesus

2Thessalonians 2:3 Let no man deceive you by any means: for that day shall not come, except there come a falling away first, and <u>that</u> man of sin be revealed, the son of perdition;

Satan

Utter destruction

The remainder of the First Epistle of John is written to Little Children

John 21:15 Feed my lambs

V.18 *L*_____ *c*_____,

V.18 It is the *l*_____ time: and as ye have heard *t*_____ antichrist shall come,

even now are there *m*_____ antichrists;
whereby *w*_____ *k*_____ that it is the last time.

V.18 Little children,

V.19 They went out from us, but they were not of us; for if they had been of us, they would no doubt have continued with us: but they *went out*, that they might be *made manifest* that they were not all of us.

antichrist

Jesus had many disciples but some turned back.

John 6:66 From that time many of his disciples went back, and walked no more with him. *When these disciples turned back, they were made manifest they were against Him.*

Matthew 12:30 He that is not with me is against me; and he that gathereth not with me scattereth abroad.

anointing

V.20 But ye have an *unction* from the *Holy One*, and *ye know all things.*
There is nothing else to know concerning the Christ other than what is written.

V.21 I have not written unto you because ye know not the truth, but *because ye know it*, and that no *lie is of the truth.* **John 14:6 Jesus saith unto him, I am the way, the truth, and the life: no man cometh unto the Father, but by me**

V.22 Who is a *liar* but he that *denieth* that *Jesus is the Christ?* He is *antichrist, that denieth the Father and the Son.*

John 2:23 Whosoever *denieth the Son*, the same *hath not the Father:* he that acknowledgeth the Son hath the Father also.

John 21:15 Feed my lambs
V.18 Little children,

V.19 They went out from us, but they were not of us; for if they had been of us, they would no doubt have continued with us: but they w_____ o_____, that they might be m_____ m_____ that they were not all of us.

John 6:66 From that time many of his disciples went back, and walked no more with him.

Matthew 12:30 He that is not with me is against me; and he that gathereth not with me scattereth abroad.

V.20 But ye have an u_____ from the H_____ O_____, and ____ k_____ a_____ t_____.

V.21 I have not written unto you because ye know not the truth, but b_____ ____ k_____ i_____, and that no l_____ is of the t_____.
John 14:6 Jesus saith unto him, I am the way, the truth, and the life: no man cometh unto the Father, but by me

V.22 Who is a l_____ but he that d_____ that J_____ ____ t_____ C_____? He is a_____, t_____ d_____ the F_____ and the S_____.

John 2:23 Whosoever d_____ the S_____, the same h_____ n_____ the F_____: he that a_____ the S_____ h_____ the F_____ a_____.

John 21:15 Feed my lambs

V.18 Little children,

(Continued...)

Begins teaching about the fellowship we have with the Father and the Son as believers.

John 1:4 And these things write we unto you, that your joy may be full.

of this epistle

abide means to remain or rest in.

V.24 Let that therefore *abide* in you, which ye have heard from the *beginning*.

abide

(fellowship)

If that which ye have heard from the beginning *shall remain in you*, ye also shall *continue in the Son, and in the Father.*

In the beginning of this epistle, John declares what the disciples have heard from the beginning of their time with Jesus.

.

John 1:1 That which was <u>from the beginning</u>, which we have heard, which we have seen with our eyes, which we have looked upon, and our hands have handled, of the Word of life;
John 1:3 That which we have seen and heard declare we unto you, that ye also<u> may have fellowship with us: and truly our fellowship is with the Father, and with his Son Jesus Christ.</u>

John 1:5 This then is the message which we have heard of him, and declare unto you, <u>that God is light, and in him is no darkness at all.</u>

V.25 And this is the promise that he hath *promised* us, even *eternal life.*

John 21:15 Feed my lambs
V.18 Little children,
(Continued...)

John 1:4 And these things write we unto you, that your joy may be full.

V.24 Let that therefore a_____ in you, which ye have heard from the b_____.

If that which ye have heard from the beginning s_____ r_____ _____ y_____, ye also shall c_____ _____ the S_____, and _____ the F_____.

John 1:1 That which was <u>from the beginning,</u> which we have heard, which we have seen with our eyes, which we have looked upon, and our hands have handled, of the Word of life;
John 1:3 That which we have seen and heard declare we unto you, that ye also<u> may have fellowship with us: and truly our fellowship is with the Father, and with his Son Jesus Christ.</u>

John 1:5 This then is the message which we have heard of him, and declare unto you, <u>that God is light, and in him is no darkness at all.</u>

V.25 And this is the promise that he hath p_____ us, even e_____ l_____.

V.18 Little children,

(Continued...)

V.26 These things have I written unto you *concerning them that seduce you.*

dwelleth

Holy Spirit

V.27 But the *anointing* which ye have received of him *abideth* in you, and *ye need not* that *any man teach you:* but as the same anointing teacheth you of *all things,* and *is truth,* and is *no lie,* and even as it hath taught you, *ye shall abide in him.*

From V. 26 this is concerning them that would seduce you. The Holy Spirit will teach us of all things of God. There is no man that has ascended up to heaven but Jesus and no man knows of heavenly things except the 3 that are in heaven. Do not let any man seduce you with fables and superstitions. No man can knows of these things.

V.28 And now, *little children, abide in him;* that, when he shall appear, we *may have confidence,* and *not be ashamed before him at his coming.*

His second coming

Not ashamed

Abide in Him (Light)   Abide in the world   Ashamed at His coming

V.29 If *ye know* that *he is righteous,* ye know that every one that *doeth righteousness is born of him.*
1 John 3:9 Whosoever is born of God doth not commit sin; <u>for his seed remaineth in him: and he cannot sin, because he is born of God.</u>

(eternal security)

V.18 Little children,
(Continued...)

V.26 These things have I written unto you c_____ t_____ that s_____ you.

V.27 But the a_____ which ye have received of him a_____ in you, and y_____ n_____ *not* that a_____ m_____ t_____ y_____: but as the same anointing teacheth you of a_____ t_____, and *is* t_____, and is n____ l____, and even as it hath taught you, y____ s_____ a_____ *in* h_____.

V.28 And now, *little* c_____, a_____ *in* h____; t_____ when he shall appear, we *may have* c_____ *and* n____ *be* a_____ b_____ *him at his coming.*

V.29 If y___ k_____ that *he is* r_____, ye know that every one that d_____ r_____ *is* b_____ *of* h_____.

Read Chapter 3

Hebrews 4:12 For the word of God is quick, and powerful, and sharper than any twoedged sword, piercing even to the dividing asunder of soul and spirit, and of the joints and marrow, and is a discerner of the thoughts and intents of the heart.

CHAPTER 3 V.1-6 Key

2:18 Little children,
(Continued...)

(6) V.5 And ye know that *he was manifested to take away our sins;* and in him is no sin.

Heaven

Jesus

(7) V.6 Whosoever *abideth* in him *sinneth not:* whosoever *sinneth* hath *not seen* him, neither *known* him.

(does not abide in Him but walks in the world)

John 1:10 He was in the world, and the world was made by him, and <u>the world knew him not</u>

absence of God

(1) V.1 Behold, what manner of *love* the Father hath bestowed upon us, that we should be called the *sons of God:*

(2) V.1 *therefore* the world *knoweth us not,* because it knew him not.

(3) V.2 ... and it doth not *yet* appear what we shall be: but we know that, when *he shall appear,* we shall be like him; for we shall see him as he is.
at His Second Coming

(5) V.4 <u>Whosoever committeth sin transgresseth also the law</u>: for *sin is the transgression of the law.*

steadfast and sure

(4) V.3 And every man that hath this *hope* in him purifieth himself, even as he is *pure.*

that He is coming again

1Peter 1:22 <u>Seeing ye have purified your souls in obeying the truth through the Spirit</u> unto unfeigned love of the brethren,

John 21:15 Feed my lambs

2:18 Little children, *(Continued...)*

6 V.5 And ye know that h___ w_____ m_____ to t_____ a_____ our s_____; and in him is no sin.

John 1:10 He was in the world, and the world was made by him, <u>and the world knew him not</u>

Jesus

Heaven

7 V.6 Whosoever a_____ in him s_____ n_____: whosoever s_____ hath n____ s_____ h_____, neither known him.

absence of God

1 V.1 Behold, what manner of *l*_____ the Father hath bestowed upon us, that we should be called the *s*_____ of *g*_____:

3 V.2 ... and it doth not *y*_____ appear what we shall be: but we know that, *w*_____ *h*___ *s*_____ *a*_____, we shall be like him; for we shall see him as he is.

4 V.3 And every man that hath this *h*_____ in him purifieth himself, even as he is *p*_____.

2 V.1 *t*_____ the world k_____ u___ n_____, ...ause it knew him not.

5 V.4 <u>Whosoever committeth sin transgresseth also the law</u>: for *s*_____ *is the t*_____ *of the l*___.

CHAPTER 3
V.7-10
Key

2:18 Little children,

abiding is fellowship
born is salvation

2

V.8 He that *committeth sin* is of the *devil;* for the devil sinneth from the beginning.

V.10 Corrupt fruit

4

V.9 Whosoever is *born of God doth not commit sin;* for *his seed remaineth in him:* and he cannot sin, because he is *born* of God.

Speaking of salvation not fellowship.

Seed

5

V.10 In this the *children of God* are manifest, and the children of the devil: whosoever doeth not righteousness is not of God, neither he that loveth not his brother.

Made manifest by their fruit.

Corrupt fruit of the devil is hatred not love

Believers

Another warning about antichrists to immature Christians.

3

V.8 For this *purpose* the Son of God was manifested, that he *might destroy the works of the devil.*

John 15:5 I am the vine, ye are the branches:

V.7 *Little children,* let *no man deceive you:* he that doeth righteousness is righteous, even as he is righteous.

1

Because it is the Holy Spirit that is within believers that is righteous

Matthew 13:40 As therefore the tares are gathered and burned in the fire; so shall it be in the end of this world.

Tares (Weeds)

True Vine

Works of the flesh

Holy Spirit

2:18 Little children, (continued)

CHAPTER 3
V.7-10

④ V.9 Whosoever
is b_____ of
God doth not

c_____
s___; for his
s_____
r_____ in
him: and he
cannot sin,
because he is
b_____ of God.

⑤ V.10 In this the c_____ of
g_____ are m_____, and the
c_____ of the d_____:
whosoever doeth not righteousness
is not of God, neither he that loveth
not his brother.

② V.8 He that
c_____
s_____ is of the
d_____; for
the devil sinneth
from the
beginning.

V.10 Corrupt fruit

③ V.8 For this
p_____
the Son of God
was manifested,
that he
m_____
d_____ the
w_____ of
the d_____.

Works of the flesh

Tares (Weeds)

John 15:5 I am the vine, ye are the branches:

True Vine

Holy Spirit

Believers

① V.7 L_____ c_____,
let n___ m_____ d_____
y_____: he that doeth
righteousness is righteous,
even as he is righteous.

2:18 Little children, (continued)

(1) V.11 For this is the message that *ye* heard from the *beginning*, that we should *love* one another.

(2) *Cain and Abel*
V.12 Not as Cain, who was of *that* wicked one, and slew his brother. And wherefore slew he him? *Because* his own works were evil, and his brother's righteous.

V.10 Corrupt fruit

(3) V.13 *Marvel not*, my brethren, if the world hate you.

Love

(4) V.14... *We know* that we have passed from death unto life, because *we love the brethren...*

it was manifested

(7) V.16 *Hereby perceive* we the love of God, *because he laid down his life* for us: and we ought to lay down our lives for the brethren.

Cain was of the devil. He was a murder who took the life of his brother. Jesus laid down His own life for us. This is love and if we abide in Christ we will love our brothers.

(5) V. 14 ...He that loveth not his brother *abideth in death*

Tares are gathered and burned at the end of the world

V.15 Whosoever *hateth* his brother is a *murderer*: and ye know that no murderer hath eternal life abiding in him.

Tares (Weeds)

Works of the flesh

John 15:5 I am the vine, ye are the branches:

Believers

True Vine

Holy Spirit

(8) V.17 But whoso hath this world's good, and seeth his brother have need, and shutteth up his bowels of compassion from him, *how dwelleth the love* of God in him?

fruit   *means to abide*
If the branch does not abide in the vine. It will wither and die.

CHAPTER 3
V.11-17

1

V.11 For this is the message that y_____ heard from the b_____, that we should l_____ o_____ a_____.

Love

2

V.12 Not as Cain, who was of t_____ wicked one, and s_____ his b_____. And wherefore slew he him? B_____ his own works were evil, and his brother's righteous.

V.10 Corrupt fruit

3

V.13 *Marvel not,* my brethren, if the world hate you.

4

V.14... W___ k_____ that we have passed from death unto life, because *we l*_____ the b_____.

5

V. 14 ...He that loveth not his brother a_____ in d_____

6

V.15 Whosoever h_____ his brother is a m_____: and ye know that no murderer hath eternal life abiding in him.

Believers

John 15:5 I am the vine, ye are the branches:

7

V.16 *Hereby perceive* we the love of God, *because he* l_____ *down his* l_____ for us: and we ought to lay down our lives for *the b*_____.

8

V.17 But whoso hath this world's good, and seeth *his b*_____ have need, and shutteth up his bowels of compassion from him, *how* d_____ the love of God in him?

Tares (Weeds)

True Vine

Works of the flesh

Holy Spirit

V.18 *My little children,* let us not love in word, neither in tongue; *but in deed and in truth.*

V.19 And *hereby we know* that we are *of the truth,* and shall *assure our hearts* before him.

Our heart tells us that we should be condemned and undeserving

The flesh makes us doubt the promises of God.

Our heart condemns us not because we have confidence in God. .

3

V.20 For *if our heart condemn us,*

4

V.20 *God is greater than our heart,* and knoweth all things.

Heaven

5

V.21 Beloved, if our heart condemn us not, then have we confidence toward God.

We can be assured that God knows we should be condemned. and nothing is hid from Him But He loves us anyway.

Not because we feel worthy, we just have faith (confidence) in His promises.

(1)

V.18 M___ l_____ c_____, let us not love in word, neither in tongue; b_____ in d_____ and in t_____.

(2) V.19 And **hereby we know** that we are *of the* t_____, and shall a_____ our h_____ before him.

(3) V.20 For *if our* h_____ c_____ us,

(4) V.20 *God is* g_____ t_____ our h_____, and knoweth all things.

Heaven

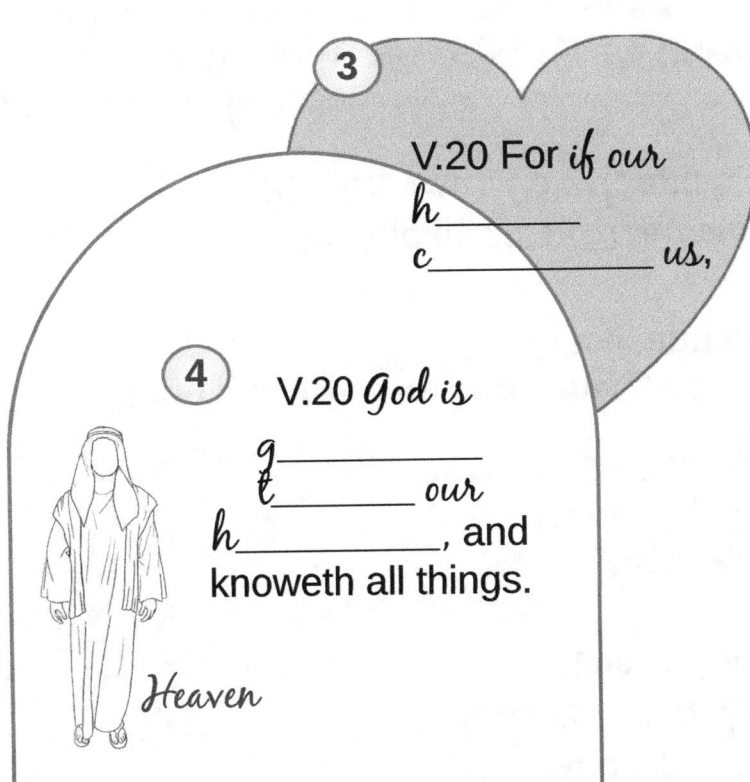

(5) V.21 Beloved, if *our* h_____ c_____ us n_____, then have we c_____ t_____ g_____.

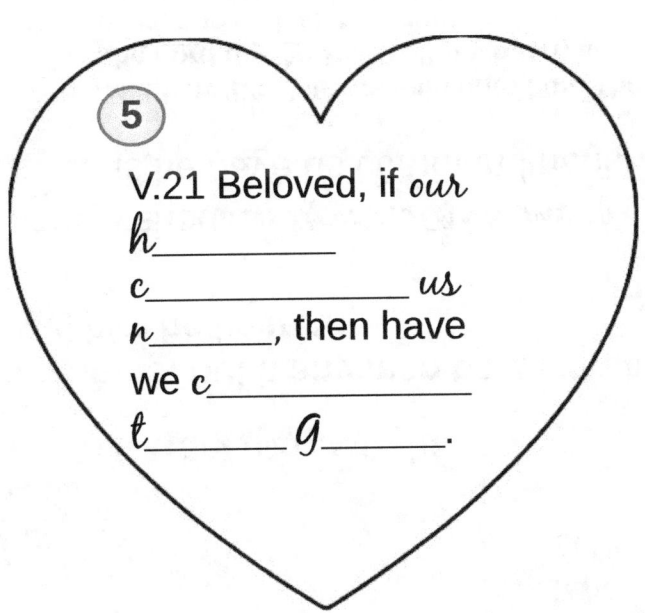

1 John 2:18 Little Children (Continued...)

V.22 And whatsoever we ask, we receive of him, *because we keep his commandments,* and do those things that are *pleasing in his sight.*

If you keep (guard) his commandments in your life, things you do will be pleasant in His sight.

Conditions to answered prayer
1. keep His commandments
2. do those things that are pleasing in His sight.

John 9:31 Now we know that God heareth not sinners: but if any man be a worshipper of God, and doeth his will, him he heareth

V.23 And this is *his commandment,* That we should *believe on the name of his Son Jesus Christ,* and *love one another,* as he gave us commandment.

His commandment
1. Believe on the name of his Son Jesus Christ. (There is no other name that you may be saved.)
2. Love one another – You will not transgress any of the 10 commandments if you Love thy God and Love your neighbor as yourself.

Matthew 22:37 Jesus said unto him, <u>Thou shalt love the Lord thy God</u> with all thy heart, and with all thy soul, and with all thy mind.
Matthew 22:38 This is the first and great commandment.
Matthew 22:39 And the second is like unto it, <u>Thou shalt love thy neighbour</u> as thyself.
Matthew 22:40 <u>On these two commandments hang all the law and the prophets.</u>

V.24 And he that *keepeth his commandments dwelleth in him,* and *he in him.* And hereby *we know* that *he abideth in us, by the Spirit* which he hath given us.

God abides in believers through the Holy Spirit

1 John 2:18 Little Children (Continued...)

V.22 And whatsoever we ask, we receive of him, b_____ w____ k_____ h____ c_____, and do those things that a____ p_____ in h_____ s_____.

John 9:31 Now we know that God heareth not sinners: but if any man be a worshipper of God, and doeth his will, him he heareth

V.23 And this is h_____ c_____, That we should b_____ on the n_____ of h_____ S_____ J_____ C_____, and l_____ o_____ a_____, as he gave us commandment.

V.24 And he that k_____ h_____ c_____ d_____ in h_____, and h___ i____ h_____. And hereby w___ k_____ that h_____ a_____ i___ u___, by the S_____ which he hath given us.

Read Chapter 4

Acts 17:11 ...they received the word with all readiness of mind, and searched the scriptures daily, whether those things were so.

CHAPTER 4
V.1
Key

Children of God

prove

V.1 Beloved, believe not every *spirit*, but *try* the *spirits* whether they are of God: *because* many *false prophets* are gone out into the world.

spirit of antichrist

CHAPTER 4
V.1

V.1 Beloved, believe not every s_____, but t_____
the s_____ whether they are of God:
b_____ many f_____
p_____ are gone out into the world.

V.2 **Hereby know ye** the Spirit of God:

V.2...Every *spirit* that confesseth that Jesus Christ is come in the flesh is of God:
V.3 And every *spirit* that confesseth not that Jesus Christ is come in the flesh is not
of God: and this is *that spirit* of antichrist, whereof ye have heard that it should
come; and even now *already is it in the world.*   *(Satan)*
*that Antichrist may not be in the
world yet but his spirit is.*

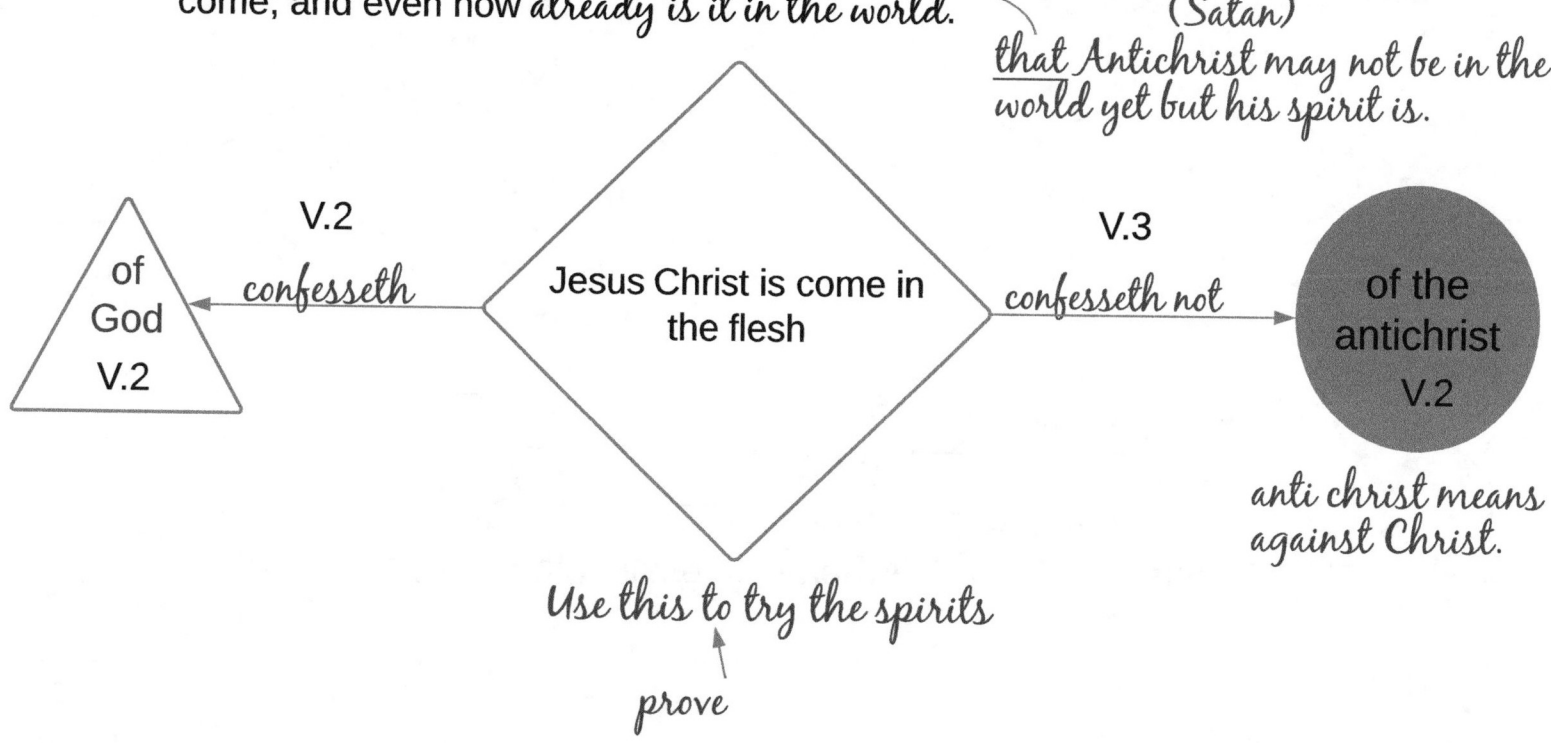

of
God
V.2

V.2
confesseth

Jesus Christ is come in
the flesh

V.3
confesseth not

of the
antichrist
V.2

*anti christ means
against Christ.*

Use this to try the spirits

prove

V.2 <u>Hereby know ye</u> the Spirit of God:

(1) V.2...Every s_____ that confesseth that Jesus Christ is come in the flesh is of God:

(3) V.3 And every s_____ that confesseth not that Jesus Christ is come in the flesh is
not of God: and this is t_____ s_____ of antichrist, whereof ye have heard
that it should come; and even now a_____ _____ i_____ i_____ the w_____.

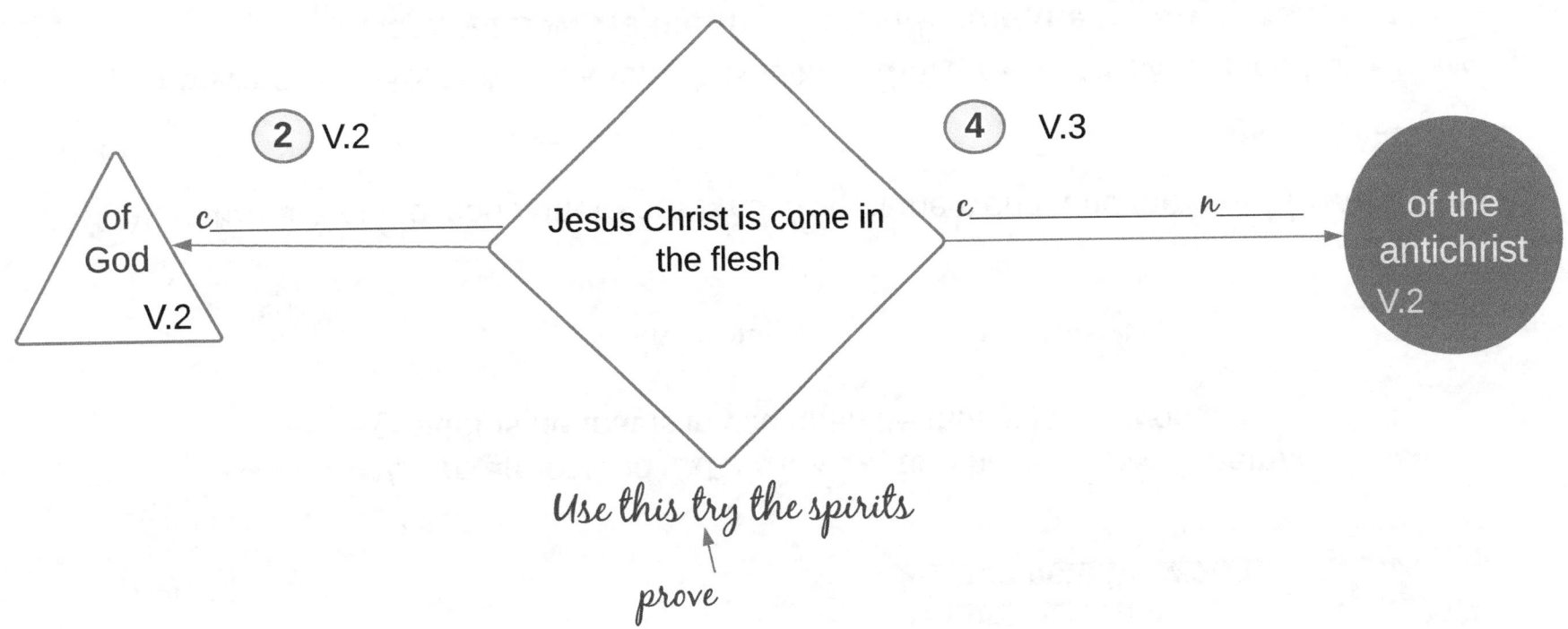

(2) V.2

of
God
c_____

V.2

Jesus Christ is come in
the flesh

(4) V.3

c_____ n_____

of the
antichrist
V.2

Use this try the spirits

prove

John 5:4 For whatsoever is <u>born of God</u> <u>overcometh the world</u>

false prophets spirits of antichrist

the saved

① V.4 Ye are of God, *little children*, and have *overcome* them: because greater is he that is in you, than he that is in the world.

Holy Spirit   *that antichrist*

false prophets

② V.5 *They* are of the world: therefore *speak they* of the world, and the *world heareth them.*

Holy Spirit

Saved   *spirit of antichrist*

③ V.6 We are of God: he that knoweth God *heareth us;* he that is *not* of God *heareth not us.*

**Hereby know we the *spirit* of *truth*, and the *spirit* of *error.*

Holy Spirit   *spirit of antichrist*

Hereby know we the spirit of truth, and the spirit of error.

Holy Spirit ④ V.6   **spirit of truth**   **YES** ← God heareth us → **NO** → **spirit of error** ⑤ V.6

John 5:4 For whatsoever is born of God overcometh the world

(1) V.4 Ye are of God, l_____ c_____, and have o_____ them: because greater is he that is in you, than he that is in the world.

(2) V.5 J_____ are of the world: therefore s_____ t_____ of the world, and the w_____ h_____ t_____.

(3) V.6 We are of God: he that knoweth God h_____ us; he that is n_____ of God h_____ n_____ us. **Hereby know we the** s_____ **of** t_____, **and the** s_____ **of** e_____.

Hereby know we the spirit of truth, and the spirit of error.

Holy Spirit

spirit of truth

(4) V.6

Y_____

God heareth us

(5) V.6

N_____

spirit of error

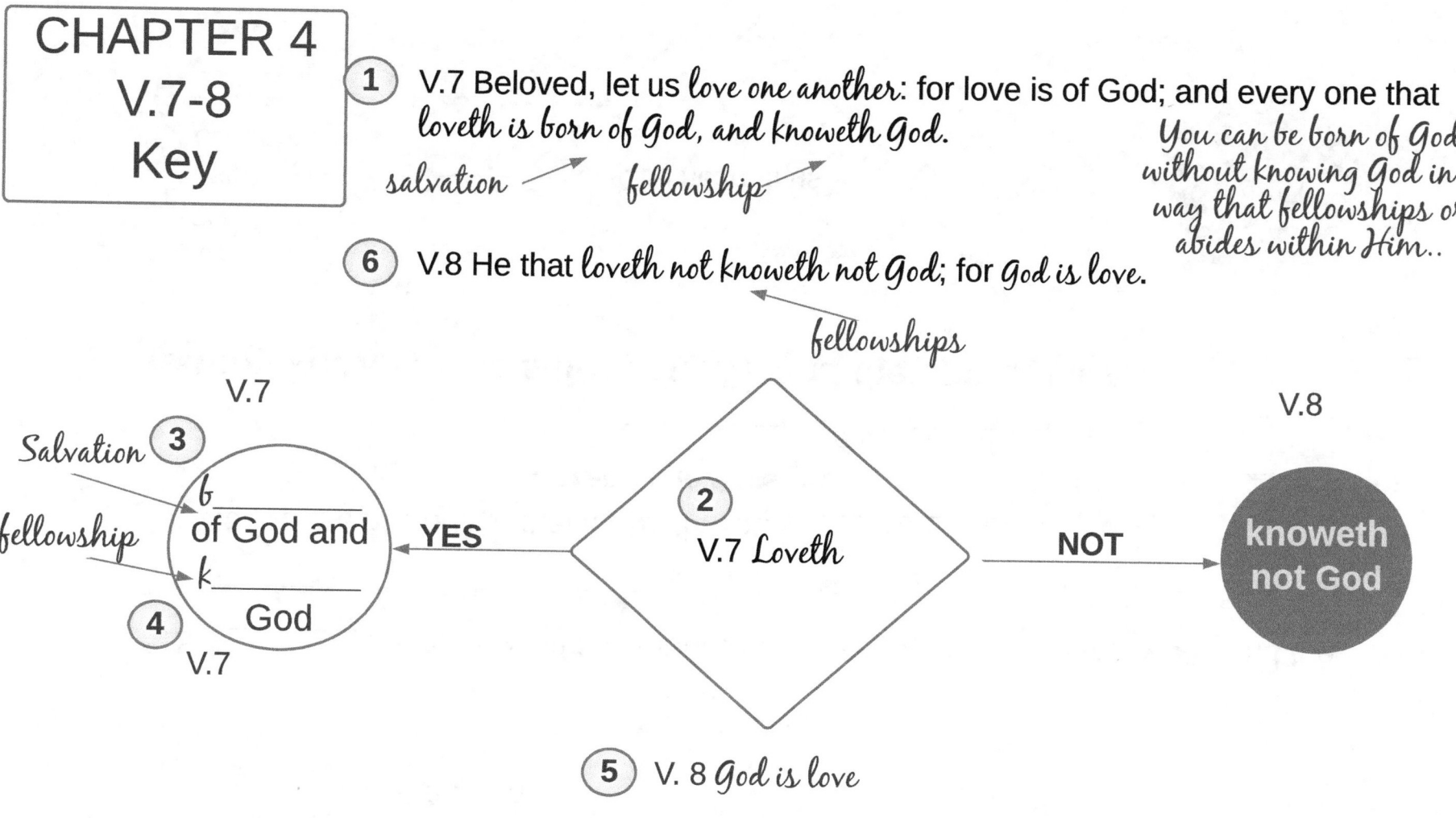

CHAPTER 4
V.7-8
Key

(1) V.7 Beloved, let us *love one another*: for love is of God; and every one that *loveth is born of God, and knoweth God.*

salvation → *fellowship* →

You can be born of God without knowing God in a way that fellowships or abides within Him..

(6) V.8 He that *loveth not knoweth not God; for God is love.*

fellowships

V.7

Salvation (3)

*b*_____ of God and *k*_____ God

(4) V.7

YES

(2) V.7 *Loveth*

NOT

knoweth not God

V.8

(5) V. 8 *God is love*

fellowship

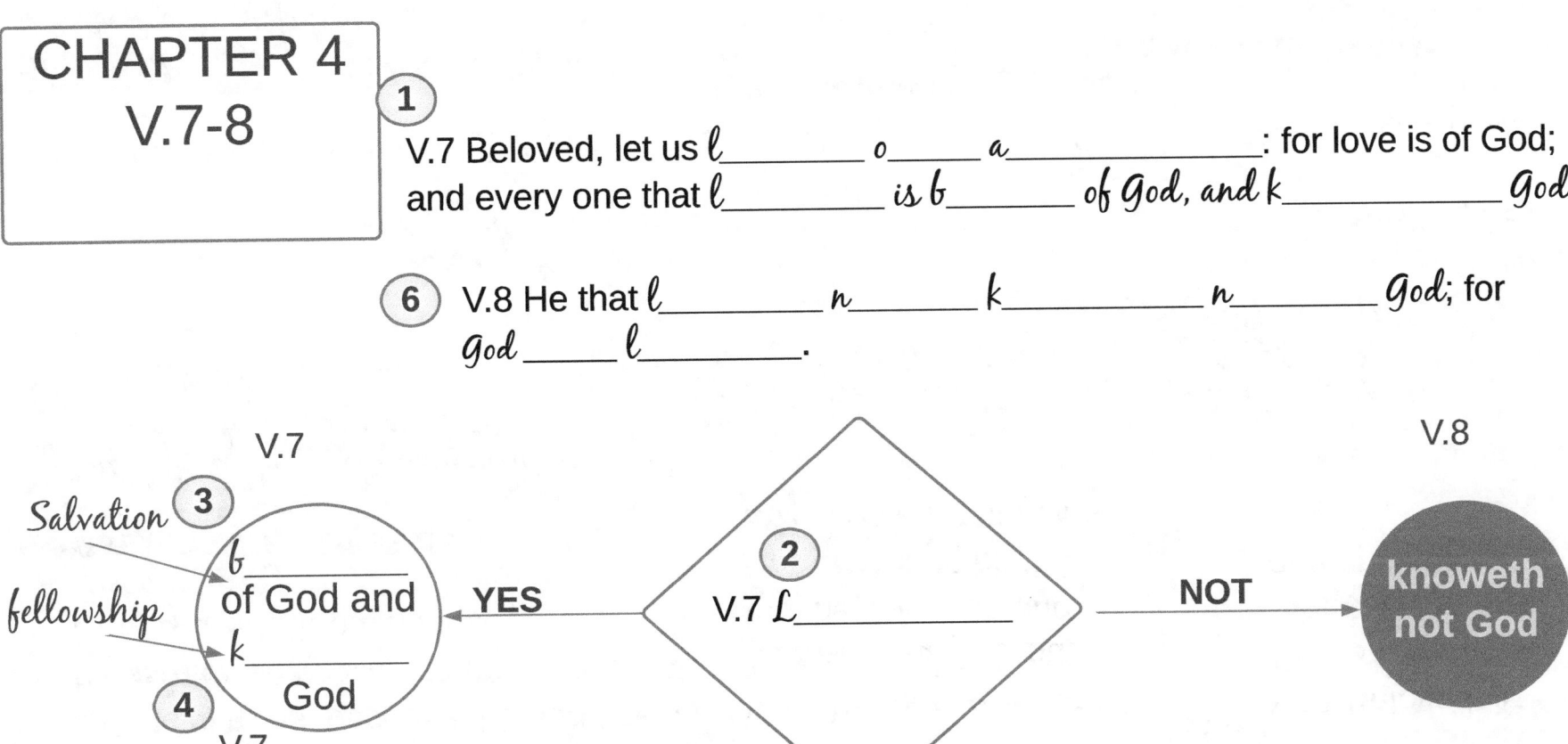

CHAPTER 4
V.7-8

(1) V.7 Beloved, let us l_____ o_____ a_____: for love is of God; and every one that l_____ is b_____ of God, and k_____ God.

(6) V.8 He that l_____ n_____ k_____ n_____ God; for God _____ l_____.

V.7

Salvation (3)

fellowship

b_____
of God and
k_____
God

(4)
V.7

YES

(2) V.7 L_____

NOT

V.8

knoweth not God

(5) V. 8 g_____ is l_____

CHAPTER 4
V.9-12
Key

Heaven

Jesus

propitiation—Lamb of God

① made plain

V.9 In this was *manifested* the love of God toward us, because that God sent his *only begotten Son* into the world, that *we might live* through him.

eternally   John 3:16 - eternal life

Without Jesus being the only begotten Son, we could have no eternal life. (See next page)

② V.10 *Herein is love, not that we loved God*, but that he loved us, and sent his *Son* to be the *propitiation* for our sins

③ V.11 Beloved, if God so loved us, we ought also to love one another.

propitiation - concile. Bring us together with God. Jesus, the Lamb of God, was sacrificed on the cross to pay for our sins and reconcile us to God

God is a Spirit...
John 4:24

The Spirit of God

④ V.12 *No man* hath *seen God* at any time. If we *love one another*, God *dwelleth in us*, and his love is *perfected in* us.

The world cannot see God, but it can see God's love manifested to its fullness in us

manifested to its fullnes

CHAPTER 4
V.9-12

Jesus

Heaven

1 V.9 In this was m_____ the love of God toward us, because that God sent his o_____ b_____ S_____ into the world, that w_____ m_____ l_____ through him.

2 V.10 H_____ is l_____, n____ t_____ w___ l_____ g_____, but that he loved us, and s_____ h____ S_____ to be the p_____ for our sins

3 V.11 Beloved, if g_____ s____ l_____ us, w_____ o_____ a_____ to love one another.

4 V.12 _____ man hath s_____ g_____ at any time. If we l_____ o_____ a_____, God d_____ ____ us, and his love is _____ _____ us.

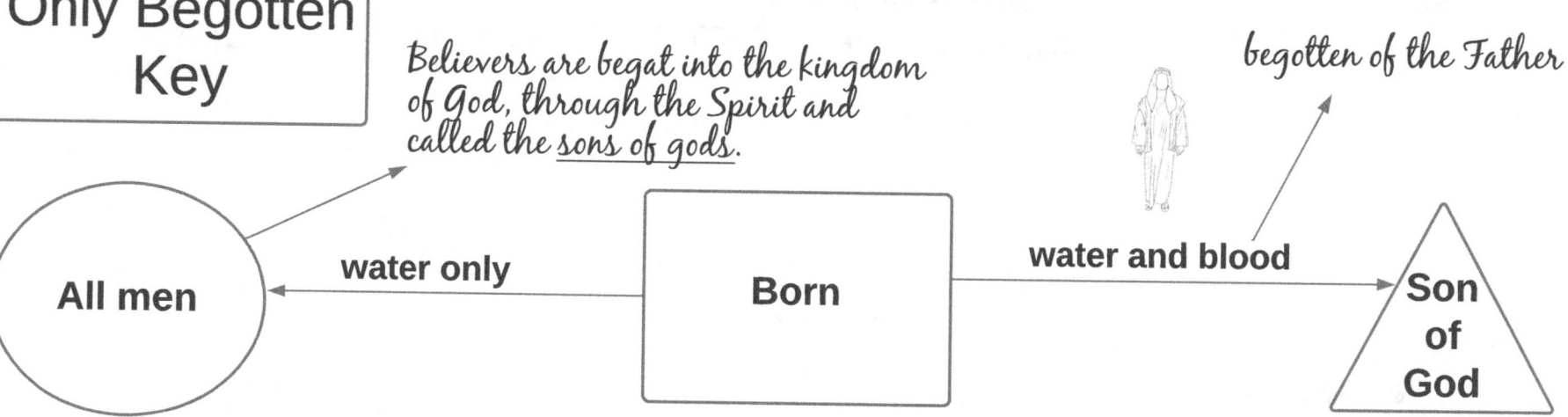

CHAPTER 4
Only Begotten
Key

Believers are begat into the kingdom of God, through the Spirit and called the <u>sons of gods</u>.

begotten of the Father

All men

water only

Born

water and blood

Son of God

John 1:12 <u>But as many as</u> received him, <u>to them gave he power to become the</u> sons of God, **even to them that believe on his name:**

John 1:13 <u>Which were born,</u> not of blood, **nor of the will of the flesh, nor of the will of man, but of God.**

James 1:18 <u>Of his own will</u> begat he us **with the word of truth, that we should be a kind of firstfruits of his creatures.**

1 John 4:9 In this was manifested the love of God toward us, because that <u>God sent</u> his only begotten Son into the world, that we might live through him.

1 John 5:6 This is he that came by water and blood, even Jesus Christ; <u>not by water only,</u> <u>but by</u> water and blood. And it is the Spirit that beareth witness, because the Spirit is truth.

Jesus, the Son of God, is the only begotten Son that has came by <u>blood and water, not water only.</u> Jesus came by water during natural childbirth through Mary. He never had an earthly father but through His virgin birth, Jesus came by the blood of the Heavenly Father.
<u>When a baby is conceived, it's blood comes solely from the father.</u> The blood of the mother never mingles with the blood of the baby. Mary's blood never mingled with that of the Saviour.

ONLY BEGOTTON SON

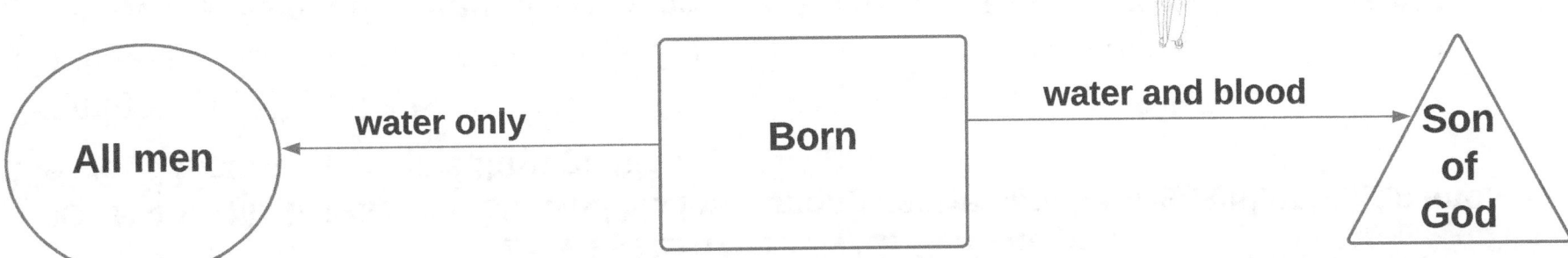

John 1:12 <u>But as many as</u> r_____ h_____, <u>to them gave he power to become the</u> s_____ of g_____, even to them that believe on his name:

John 1:13 <u>Which were born,</u> n_____ of b_____, nor of the will of the flesh, nor of the will of man, but of God.

James 1:18 <u>Of his own will</u> b_____ h____ u___ with the word of truth, that we should be a kind of firstfruits of his creatures.

1 John 4:9 In this was manifested the love of God toward us, because that <u>God sent</u> h____ o_____ b_____ S_____ into the world, that we might live through him.

1 John 5:6 This is he that came by water and blood, even Jesus Christ; <u>not by water only, but by</u> w_____ and b_____. And it is the Spirit that beareth witness, because the Spirit is truth.

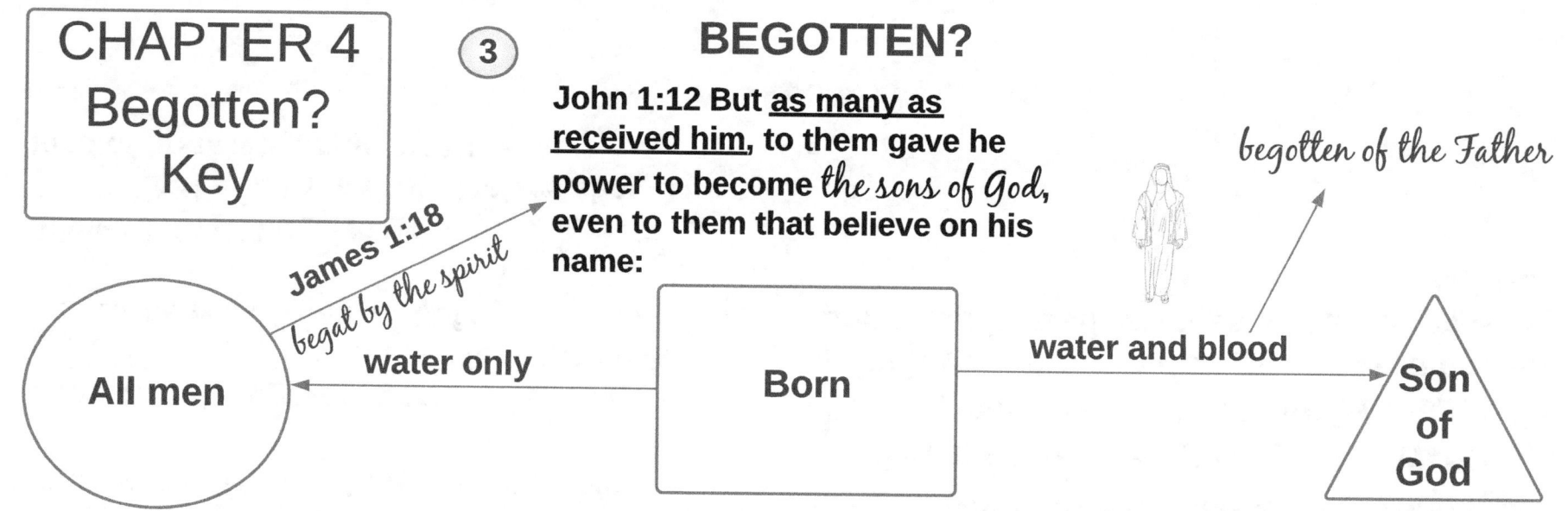

CHAPTER 4
Begotten?
Key

③

BEGOTTEN?

John 1:12 But <u>as many as</u> <u>received him</u>, to them gave he power to become *the sons of God,* **even to them that believe on his name:**

begotten of the Father

James 1:18
begat by the spirit

All men ←——— water only ——— **Born** ——— water and blood ——→ **Son of God**

KING JAMES BIBLE

① **1 JOHN 4:9 In this was manifested the love of God toward us, because that God sent his only** *begotten* **Son into the world, that we might live through him.**

NEW INTERNATIONAL VERSION

omits begotten

② **1 JOHN 4:9 This is how God showed his love among us: He sent his <u>one and only Son</u> into the world that we might live through him.**

Examine 1 JOHN 4:9 NIV
(1) If Jesus was God's one and only Son, then we are not sons of Gods and were not <u>begat by the Spirit</u> unto eternal life. **John 1:12, 1 John 3:1, Romans 8:14,19 etc. (James 1:18)**

(1) Omitting only begotten is denying the virgin birth and that Jesus was begotten by blood of the Father and not water only. Begotten is also omitted in many other verses in the NIV. **John 3:16, 1 John 4:9, etc.**
This spirit confesseth not that Jesus Christ has come in the flesh. He is merely man. .

③

BEGOTTEN?

John 1:12 But <u>as many as received him,</u> to them gave he power to become *the*

s_____ *of* G_____, even to them that believe on his name:

begotten of the Father

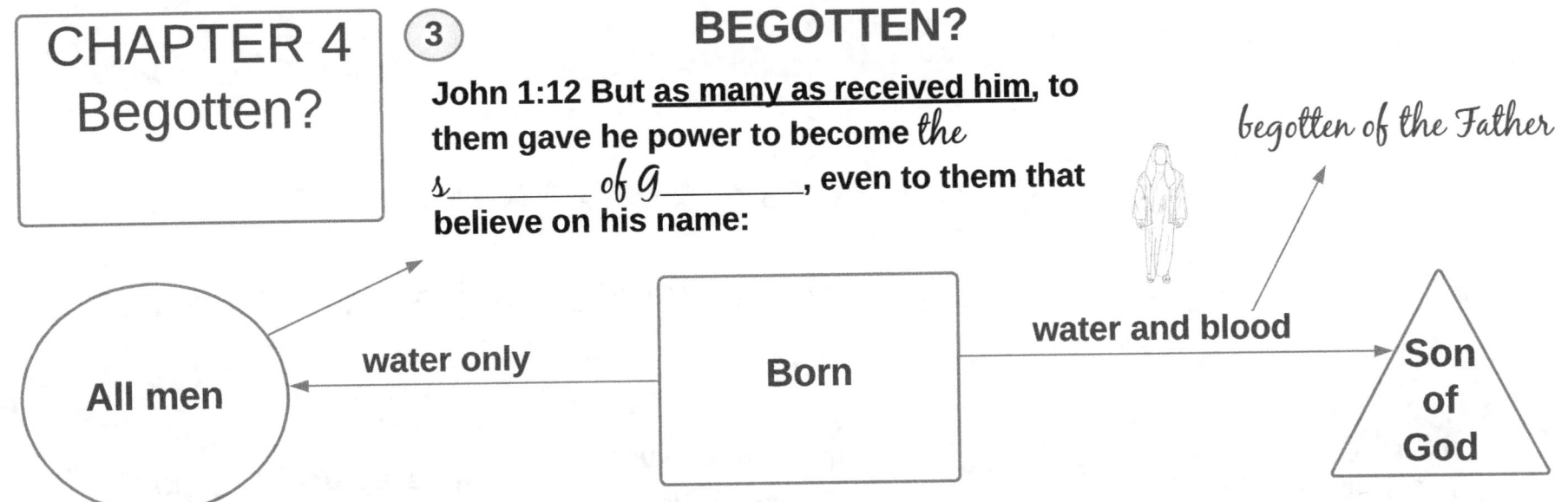

All men

water only ⟶ Born ⟶ water and blood ⟶ Son of God

KING JAMES BIBLE

① 1 JOHN 4:9 In this was manifested the love of God toward us, because that God sent his only *b*_____ Son into the world, that we might live through him.

NEW INTERNATIONAL VERSION

② 1 JOHN 4:9 This is how God showed his love among us: He sent his <u>**one and only Son**</u> into the world that we might live through him.

Disciples

abide

V.13 Hereby know we that we dwell in him, and he in us, because he hath given us of his Spirit.

Try the spirit

(1)

V.14 And we have *seen* and do *testify* that the Father *sent* the *Son to be the Saviour* of the world.

V.2 Hereby know ye the Spirit of God:

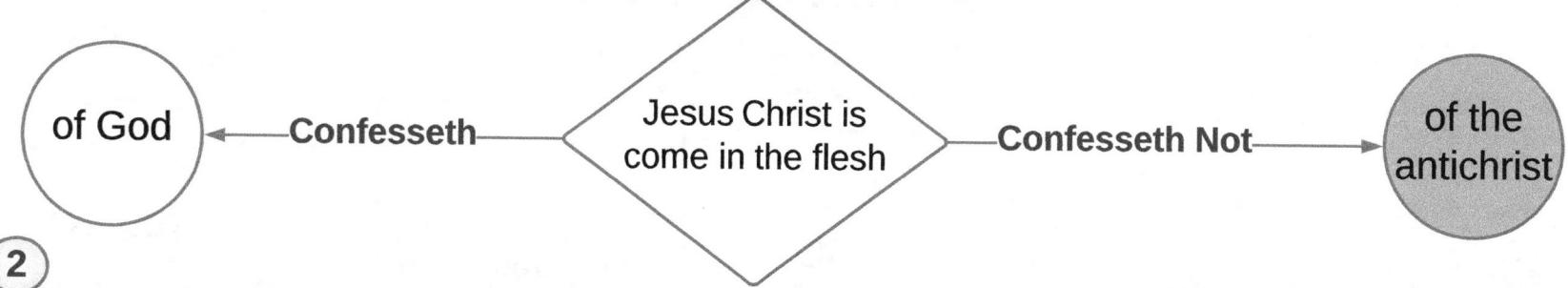

(2)

V. 15 Whosoever shall *confess that Jesus is the Son of God, God dwelleth in him, and he in God.*

Conclusion: The Disciples have the Spirit of God and are not false prophets.

V.13 <u>Hereby know we</u> that we dwell in him, and he in us, because he hath given us of his Spirit.

(1)

V.14 And we have s_____ and do t_____ that the Father s_____ the S_____ to be the S_____ of the world.

V.2 <u>Hereby know ye</u> the Spirit of God:

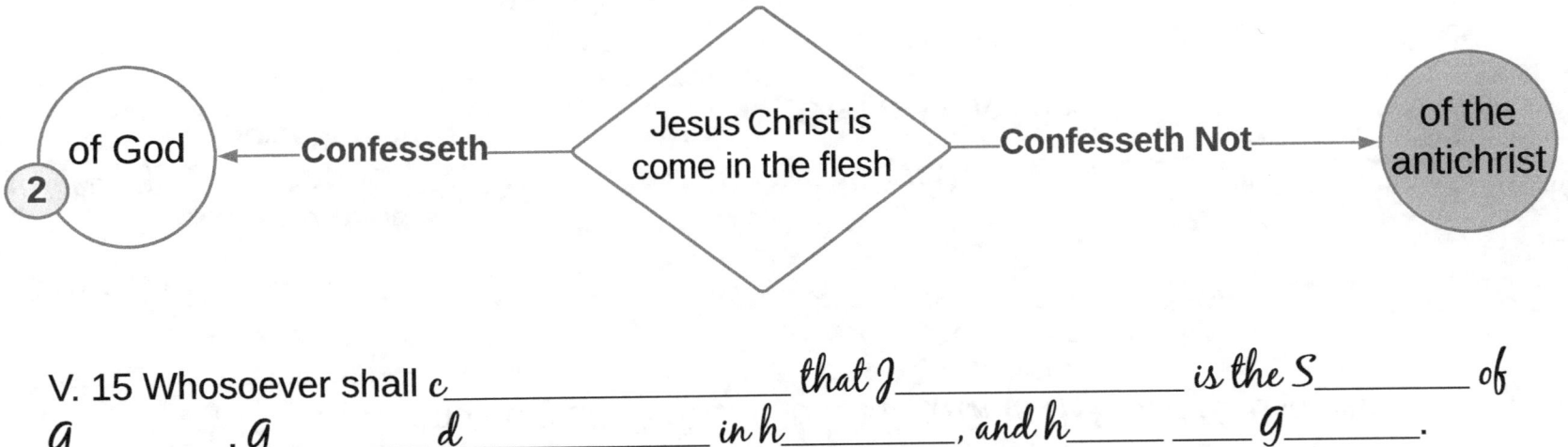

of God ←—Confesseth— ◇ Jesus Christ is come in the flesh ◇ —Confesseth Not—→ of the antichrist

(2)

V. 15 Whosoever shall c_____ that J_____ is the S_____ of g_____, g_____ d_____ in h_____, and h_____ _____ g_____.

CHAPTER 4
V.16-18
Key

1 V.16 And we have *known and believed* the love that God hath to us. *God is love;* and he that *dwelleth in love dwelleth in God,* and God in him.

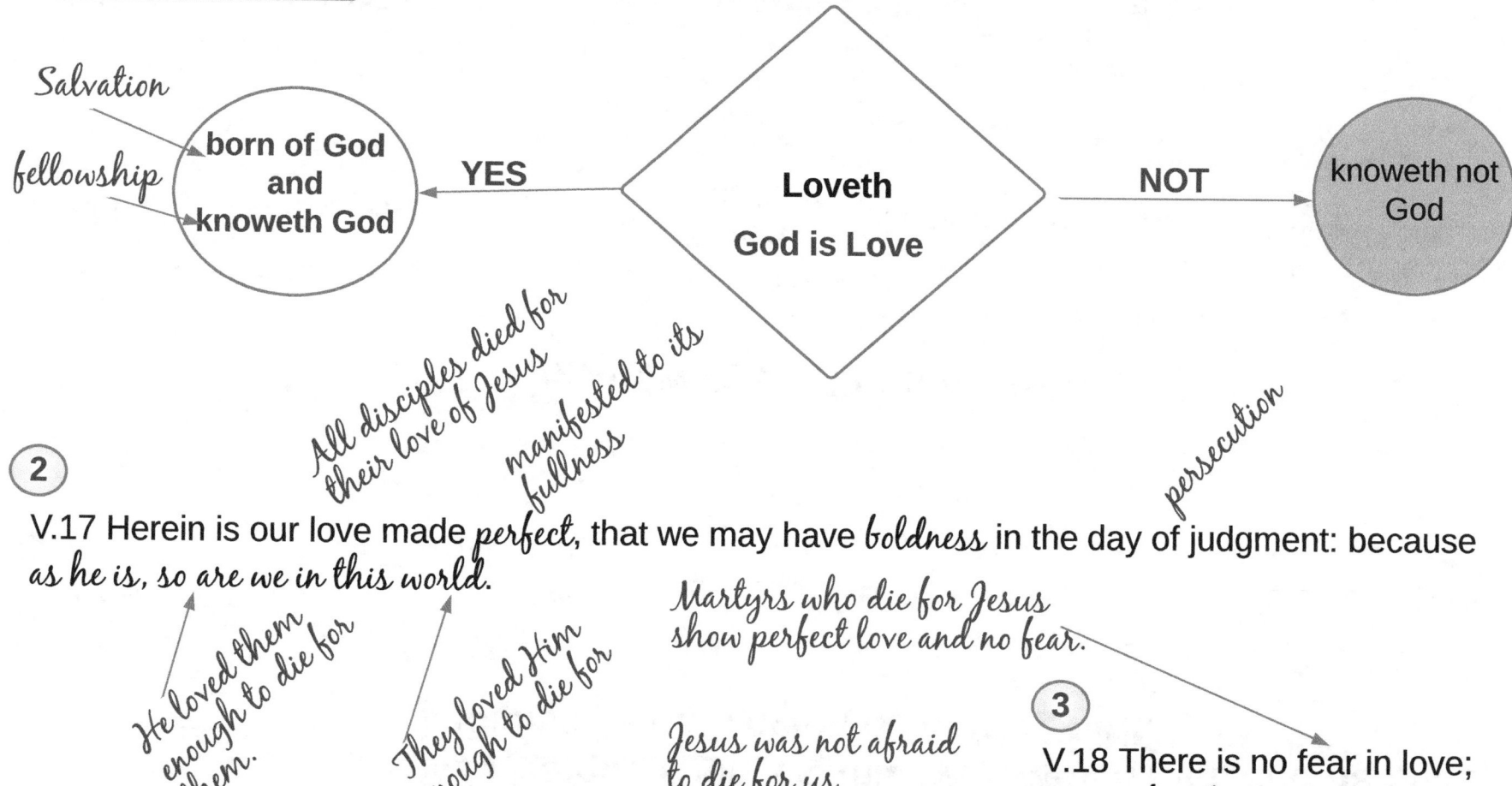

Salvation

fellowship

born of God and knoweth God

YES ← **Loveth God is Love** NOT → knoweth not God

2

All disciples died for their love of Jesus

manifested to its fullness

persecution

V.17 Herein is our love made *perfect,* that we may have *boldness* in the day of judgment: because *as he is, so are we in this world.*

He loved them enough to die for them.

They loved Him enough to die for Him.

Martyrs who die for Jesus show perfect love and no fear.

Jesus was not afraid to die for us.

3

Love manifested to its fullness

V.18 There is no fear in love; but *perfect love* casteth out fear: because fear hath torment. He that feareth is not made perfect in love.

CHAPTER 4
V.16-18

(1) V.16 And we have k_____ and b_____ the love that God hath to us. G_____ is l_____; and he that d_____ in l_____ d_____ in g_____, and God in him.

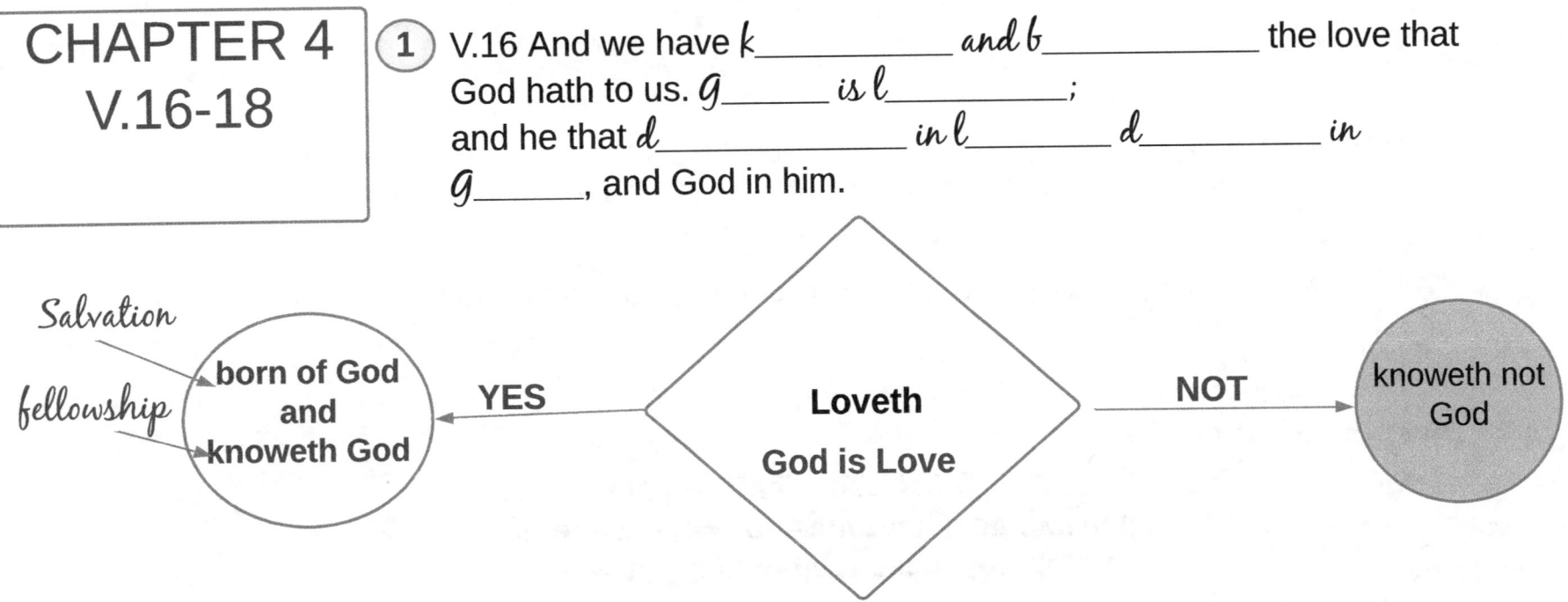

Salvation

fellowship

born of God and knoweth God

YES

Loveth

God is Love

NOT

knoweth not God

(2)

V.17 Herein is our love made p_____, that we may have b_____ in the day of judgment: because____ h_____ is, s____ a_____ w____ ____t_____ w_____.

(3) V.18 There is n___ b_____ in love; but p_____ l_____ casteth out fear: because fear hath torment. He that feareth is not made perfect in love.

V.19 We love him, because he *first loved us.*

**John 4:10 Herein is love, not that
we loved God, <u>but that he loved
us</u>, and sent his Son to be the
propitiation for our sins**

V.20 If a man say, I love God, and *hateth his brother, he is a liar:* for he that loveth
not his brother whom he hath seen, how can he love God *whom he hath not seen?*

**John 4:12 No man hath seen God at any
time. If we love one another, God dwelleth
in us, and his <u>love is perfected in us.</u>**

*manifested to its
fullness*

V.21 And this commandment have we from him, That he who *loveth God love his brother also.*

*When we love God, which cannot be seen because He is a Spirit, He dwells within us.
Others can see Him when we love one another and His love is manifested to its fullness.*

V.19 We love him, because he f_____
l_____ _____.

**John 4:10 Herein is love, not that
we loved God, <u>but that he loved
us</u>, and sent his Son to be the
propitiation for our sins**

V.20 If a man say, I love God, and h_____ h_____ b_____, h____ is a
l_____: for he that loveth not his brother whom he hath seen, how can he
love God w_____ h_____ h_____ n_____ s_____?

**John 4:12 No man hath seen God at any
time. If we love one another, God dwelleth
in us, and his <u>love is perfected in us.</u>**

Read Chapter 5

Acts 17:11 ...they received the word with all readiness of mind, and searched the scriptures daily, whether those things were so.

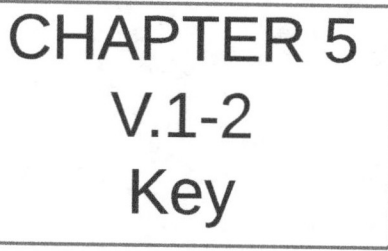

CHAPTER 5
V.1-2
Key

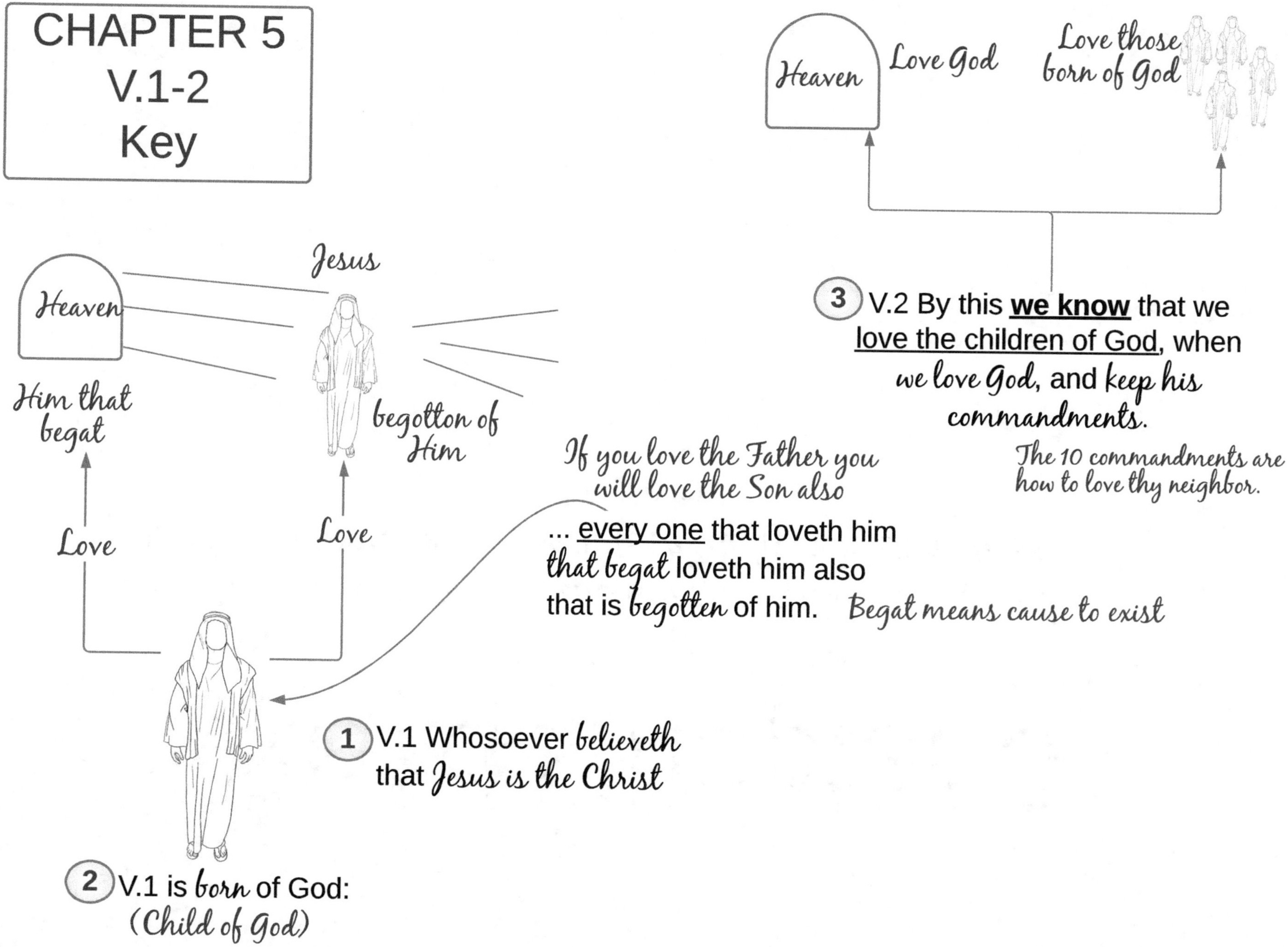

Heaven   Love God   Love those born of God

③ V.2 By this **we know** that we love the children of God, when we love God, and keep his commandments.

The 10 commandments are how to love thy neighbor.

Jesus

Heaven

Him that begat

begotton of Him

Love   *Love*

If you love the Father you will love the Son also

... every one that loveth him that begat loveth him also that is begotten of him.   *Begat means cause to exist*

① V.1 Whosoever *believeth* that *Jesus is the Christ*

② V.1 is *born* of God:
(Child of God)

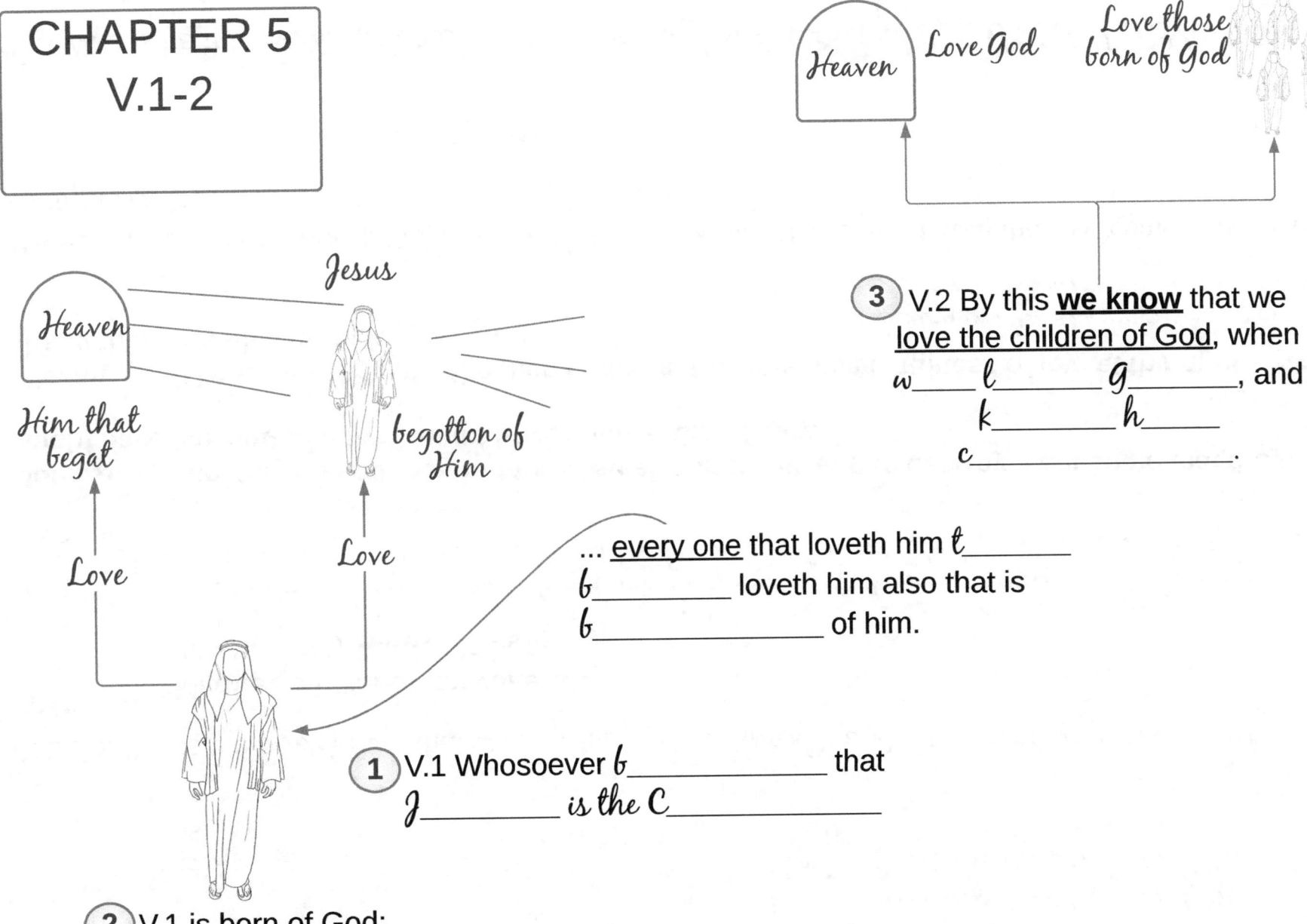

CHAPTER 5
V.1-2

Heaven   Love God   Love those
born of God

Jesus

Heaven

Him that
begat

begotton of
Him

Love   Love

3 V.2 By this **we know** that we
<u>love the children of God</u>, when
w____ l_____ g_____, and
k_____ h____
c_____.

... <u>every one</u> that loveth him t_____
b_____ loveth him also that is
b_____ of him.

1 V.1 Whosoever b_____ that
J_____ is the C_____

2 V.1 is born of God:

Child of God — Born of God and has overcome the world through faith in the blood of Jesus Christ which cleanseth us from all sin.

V.3 For this is the *love of God*, that we *keep his commandments*: and his commandments are *not grievous*.

Matthew 11:30 For my yoke is easy, and my burden is light.

We are pleased to keep His commandments. They bring blessings to our life in contrast to sin which brings despair. The love of God is not that we have eternal life but we can also have life more abundantly on earth.

John 10:10 The thief cometh not, but for to steal, and to kill, and to destroy: I am come that they might have life, and that they might have it more abundantly.

Psalm 16:11 Thou wilt shew me the path of life: in thy presence is fulness of joy; at thy right hand there are pleasures for evermore.

abiding in Him through the keeping of His commandments

V.4 For whatsoever is *born of God overcometh the world*: and this is the *victory* that overcometh the world, even *our faith*.

We are save by grace through faith.

V.5 Who is he that *overcometh* the world, but he that *believeth that Jesus is the Son of God?*

Child of God

V.3 For this is the l_____ of g_____, that we k_____ h_____ c_____: and his commandments are n_____ g_____.

Matthew 11:30 For my yoke is easy, and my burden is light.

John 10:10 The thief cometh not, but for to steal, and to kill, and to destroy: I am come that they might have life, and that they might have it more abundantly.

V.4 For whatsoever is b_____ of g_____ o_____ the w_____: and this is the v_____ that overcometh the world, even o_____ f_____.

V.5 Who is he that o_____ the world, but he that b_____ that J_____ is the S_____ of g_____?

Child of God

means which is

V.6 This is he that came by *water and blood, even Jesus Christ; not by water only,* but by **water and blood**. And *it is the Spirit that beareth witness, because the Spirit is truth.*

children of God
sons of God

Jesus is the only begotten Son that came by water and blood. Not water only

Through the virgin birth His blood is not tainted with sin from man. Jesus inherited His Sonship from the Heavenly Father.

Jesus Christ

John 1:12 But as many as received him, to them gave he power <u>to become the sons of God, even to them that believe on his name:</u>

John 1:13 Which were born, <u>not of blood,</u> nor of the will of the flesh, nor of the will of man, but of God.

can't be inherited like Jesus who inherited it from the blood of the Father nor can we inherit it from our earthly fathers.

The Spirit bear witness of this truth to the soldier at the cross.

John 19:34 But one of the soldiers with a spear pierced his side, <u>and forthwith came there out blood and water.</u>

John 19:35 And he that saw it, <u>bare record</u> and his record is true: and he knoweth that he saith true, <u>that ye might believe</u>.

We get our blood from our earthly father whose blood is tainted with sin from Adam. What we did inherit was condemnation.

Romans 5:12 Wherefore, as <u>by one man sin entered into the world,</u> and death by sin; and <u>so death passed upon all men,</u> for that all have sinned:

Child of God

(or = to)

V.6 This is he that came by w_____ and b_____, e_____ J_____ C_____;
n_____ by w_____ o_____, but by water and blood. And i_____ i_____ t_____
S_____ that b_____ w_____, b_____ t_____ S_____ i___
t_____.

children of God

Jesus Christ

John 19:34 But one of the soldiers with a spear pierced his side, <u>and forthwith came there out blood and water.</u>
John 19:35 And he that saw it, <u>bare record</u> and his record is true: and he knoweth that he saith true, <u>that ye might believe</u>.

1 John 4:2 Hereby know ye the Spirit of God:

of God ⟵Confesseth⟵ Jesus Christ is come in the flesh ⟶Confesseth Not⟶ of the antichrist

..Heb. 9:12 ...and without shedding of blood is no remission.

Any man can be baptized in water and die on the cross. That does not give him the power to save the world from their sins!!!

KING JAMES BIBLE 1 John 5:6-8

John 5:6 This is he that came by water and blood, even Jesus Christ; not by water only, but by water and blood. And it is the Spirit that beareth witness, because the Spirit is truth.

John 5:7 For there are three that bear record in heaven, the Father, the Word, and the Holy Ghost: and these three are one.

John 5:8 And there are three that bear witness in earth, the Spirit, and the water, and the blood: and these three agree in one.

NEW INTERNATIONAL READER'S VERSION 1st John 5:6-8

V.6 Jesus Christ is the one who was baptized in water and died on the cross. He wasn't just baptized in water. He also died on the cross. The Holy Spirit has given a truthful witness about him. That's because the Spirit is the truth. V.7 There are three that give witness about Jesus.V.8They are the Holy Spirit, the baptism of Jesus and his death. And the three of them agree.

NO!!!

Jesus did not come in the flesh through the baptism of John the Baptist. This is not confessing Jesus came in the flesh! It is His coming by water of the virgin birth with the blood of the Heavenly Father that saves us. .

Matthew 4:4 ... It is written, Man shall not live by bread alone, but by every word that proceedeth out of the mouth of God. *We must have every word or false doctrine is allowed to creep in.*

TRY The spirit of the New International Reader's Version

1 John 4:2 Hereby know ye the Spirit of God:

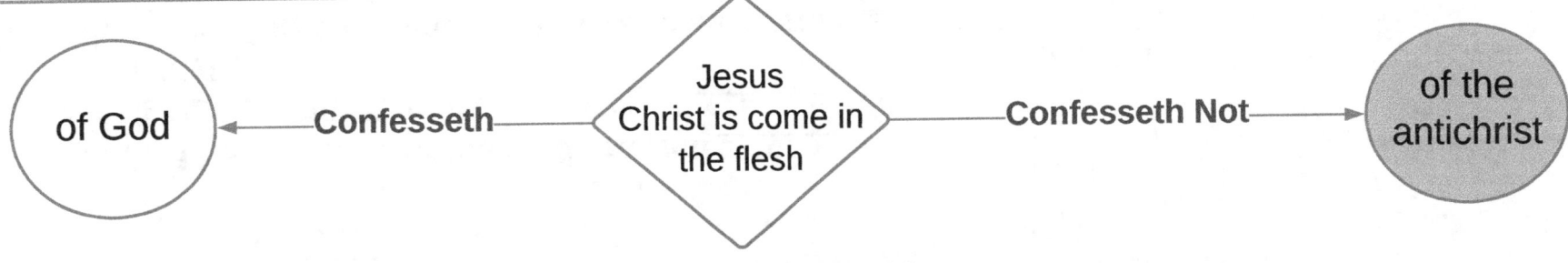

of God ←——Confesseth——— Jesus Christ is come in the flesh ———Confesseth Not——→ of the antichrist

TRY THE SPIRITS

KING JAMES BIBLE 1 JOHN 5:6-8

John 5:6 This is he that came by water and blood, even Jesus Christ; <u>not by water only, but by water and blood.</u> And it is the Spirit that beareth witness, because the Spirit is truth.

John 5:7 For there are three that bear record in heaven, the Father, the Word, and the Holy Ghost: and these three are one.

John 5:8 And there are three that bear witness in earth, <u>the Spirit, and the water, and the blood:</u> and these three agree in one.

NEW INTERNATIONAL READER'S VERSION 1JOHN 5:6-8

V.6Jesus <u>Christ is the one who was baptized in water and died on the cross. He wasn't just baptized in water. He also died on the cross.</u> The Holy Spirit has given a truthful witness about him. That's because the Spirit is the truth. V.7There are three that give witness about Jesus. V.8They are the <u>Holy Spirit</u>, <u>the baptism of Jesus and his death</u>. And the three of them agree.

Heaven

Jesus

① V. 7 For there are three that bear record in heaven, *the Father, the Word, and the Holy Ghost:* and these *three are* one.

All three are one so they all bare one record.

② V.8 And there are three that bear witness in earth, *the Spirit, and the water, and the blood:* and these *three agree in* one.

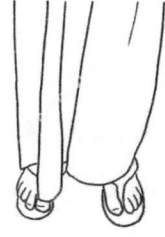

The soldier

John 19:34 But one of the soldiers with a spear pierced his side, and forthwith came there out blood and water.
John 19:35 And he that saw it bare record, and his record is true: and he knoweth that he saith true, that ye might believe.

We should believe the testimony of the Word of God is stronger than that of the soldier. But the soldier who pierced Jesus gives the witness of man that it is true.

V.9 If we receive the *witness of men,* the witness of God is greater: for this is the witness of God which he hath testified of his Son.

Heaven

1 V. 7 For there are three that bear record in heaven, *the* F_____, *the* W_____, *and the* H_____ G_____: and these three are one.

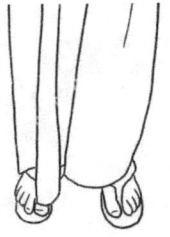

2 V.8 And there are three that bear witness in earth, *the* S_____, *and the* w_____, *and the* b_____: and these three agree in one.

John 19:34 But one of the soldiers with <u>a spear</u> <u>pierced his side, and forthwith came there out blood</u> <u>and water.</u>
John 19:35 And he that saw it bare record, and <u>his</u> <u>record is true</u>: and he knoweth that he saith true, <u>that ye might believe.</u>

V.9 If we receive the *w*_____ *of* *m*_____, the witness of God is greater: for this is the witness of God which he hath testified of his Son.

CHAPTER 5
V.10-13
Key

child of God

Holy Spirit that bears witness

V.10 He that *believeth* on the Son of God hath the *witness* in himself:

he that *believeth not* God hath made him *a liar*; because he believeth not the *record* that God gave of his Son.

Heaven

Hath means we have it now. Not that we may receive it after we die. We have eternal life now. This is eternal security.

V.11 And this is the record

If you don't believe God's record of Jesus you are calling God a liar.

V.12 *He that hath the Son hath life*; and he that hath not the Son of God hath not life.

eternal life

We must read the Bible!!

Without the Bible those who never saw or heard the Word, (Jesus Christ in the flesh) would not know we have eternal life or even believe that Jesus is the Son of God.

that God hath given to us *eternal life*, and this *life is in his Son*.

God gave us this record of His Son so that we may know we have eternal life.

V.13 These things have I written unto you that believe on the name of the Son of God; that **ye may know** that *ye have eternal life*, and that ye may believe on the name of the Son of God.

CHAPTER 5
V.10-13

V.10 He that b_____ on the Son of God hath the
w_____ in himself:

he that b_____ n_____ God hath made him a l_____;
because he believeth not the r_____ that God gave of his Son.

Heaven

V.11 And this is the record

V.12 He t_____ h_____ the
S_____ h_____ l_____;
and he that hath not the Son of
God hath not life.

that God hath given
to us e_____
l_____, and this
l_____ is in
h_____ S_____.

V.13 These things have I written unto you that believe on the name of the Son of God; that **ye may
know** that y____ h_____ e_____ l_____, and that ye may believe on the name of
the Son of God.

CHAPTER 5
V.14-19
Key

assurance

V.14 And this is the confidence that we have in him, that, if we ask any thing *according to his will*, he *heareth us*:

John 15:7 <u>If ye abide in me, and my words abide in you,</u> ye shall ask what ye will, and it shall be done unto you.

V.15 And if **we know** that he hear us, whatsoever we ask, we know that we have the *petitions* that we desired of him.

a formal request

James 5:14 Is any sick among you? let him call for the elders of the church; and let them pray over him, anointing him with oil in the name of the Lord: **James 5:15** And the prayer of faith shall save the sick, and the Lord shall raise him up; and <u>if he have committed sins, they shall be forgiven him.</u>

V.16 If any man see his brother sin a sin which is not unto death, he shall ask, and *he shall give him life* for them that sin not unto death. There is a sin unto death: I do not say that he shall pray for it.

They have been forgiven.

V.17 All unrighteousness is sin: and there is a *sin not unto death.*

His seed remaineth in Him, **John 3:9**

V.18 **We know** that *whosoever is born of God sinneth not*; but he that is <u>begotten</u> of God keepeth himself, and that wicked one toucheth him not.

Jesus can keep Himself from sin. But our sin, is not imputed to us through faith in the blood of Christ.

V.14 And this is the confidence that we have in him, that, if we ask any thing a_____ to h_____ w_____, he h_____ us:

V.15 And if **we know** that he hear us, whatsoever we ask, we know that we have the p_____ that we desired of him.

V.16 If any man see his brother sin a sin which is not unto death, he shall ask, and h____ s_____ g_____ h_____ l_____ for them that sin not unto death. There is a sin unto death: I do not say that he shall pray for it.

V.17 A_____ u_____ is s_____: and there is a s_____ n_____ unto d_____.

V.18 **We know** that w_____ is b_____ of g_____ s_____ n_____; but he that is begotten of God keepeth himself, and that wicked one toucheth him not.

Jesus
The true light John 1:9
The true vine John 15:1
True bread John 6:32

V.19 And **we know** that <u>we are of God</u>, and the *whole world lieth in wickedness.*

Jesus

V.20 And **we know** that the <u>Son of God</u> *is come,* and hath given us an understanding,

Father   *Jesus*   *means which is*

that **we may know** him that is true, and we are **<u>in him</u>** that is true, *even in* his Son Jesus Christ.

Father   *Jesus*

This **is** the true God, and eternal life.

John 17:1 These words spake Jesus, and lifted up his eyes to heaven, and said, <u>Father,</u> the hour is come; glorify thy Son, that thy Son also may glorify thee:
John 17:2 As thou hast given him power over all flesh, that he should give eternal life to as many as thou hast given him.
John 17:3 And this is life eternal, that they might know <u>thee the only true God</u>, and Jesus Christ, whom thou hast sent.

John 1:2 (For the <u>life was manifested</u>, and <u>we have seen it</u>, and <u>bear witness</u>, and <u>shew unto you that eternal life</u>, <u>which was with the Father,</u> and <u>was manifested unto us</u>;)

V.19 And **we know** that <u>we are of God</u>, and the _w_____ _w_____ _l_____ _in_

_w_____.

V.20 And **we know** that the <u>Son of God</u> _is c_____, and hath given us an understanding,

that **we may know** him that is true, and we are **<u>in him</u>** that is true, _e_____ _i_____ his Son Jesus
Christ.

This **is** the true God, and eternal life.

John 17:1 These words spake Jesus, and lifted up his eyes to heaven, and said,
<u>Father</u>, the hour is come; glorify thy Son, that thy Son also may glorify thee:
John 17:2 As thou hast given him power over all flesh, that he should give
eternal life to as many as thou hast given him.
John 17:3 And this is life eternal, that they might know<u> thee the only true God,</u>
and Jesus Christ, whom thou hast sent.

John 1:2 (For the <u>life was manifested</u>, and <u>we have seen it</u>, and<u> bear witness</u>, and <u>shew unto you</u>
<u>that eternal life</u>, <u>which was with the Father</u>, and <u>was manifested unto us</u>;)

John 5:19 And we know that we are of God, and the whole world lieth in wickedness.

John 5:20 And we know that the Son of God is come, and hath given us an understanding, that we may know him that is true, and we are in him that is true, even in his Son Jesus Christ. This is the true God, and eternal life.

lambs

John 5:21 *Little children,* keep yourselves from idols. Amen.

Any thing on which we set our affections; that to which we indulge an excessive and sinful attachment.

John 2:14 I have written unto you, fathers, because ye have known him that is from the beginning. I have written unto you, <u>young men, because ye are strong, and the word of God abideth in you, and ye have overcome the wicked one.</u> <u>John 2:15 Love not the world, neither the things that are in the world.</u> If any man love the world, the love of the Father is not in him.

Little children grow into young men becoming sheep instead of lambs. After being taught of the True Father and eternal life with the sincere milk of the word, they are instructed to keep themselves from idols. (worldly gods).

John 5:19 And we know that we are of God, and the whole world lieth in wickedness.

John 5:20 And we know that the Son of God is come, and hath given us an understanding, that we may know him that is true, and we are in him that is true, even in his Son Jesus Christ. This is the true God, and eternal life.

John 5:21 *L*_____ *c*_____, keep yourselves from idols. Amen.

John 2:14 I have written unto you, fathers, because ye have known him that is from the beginning. I have written unto you, <u>young men, because ye are strong, and the word of God abideth in you, and ye have overcome the wicked one. John 2:15 Love not the world, neither the things that are in the world.</u> If any man love the world, the love of the Father is not in him.

Little children grow into young men becoming sheep instead of lambs. After being taught of the True Father and eternal life with the sincere milk of the word, they are instructed to keep themselves from idols. (worldly gods).

Read II John

Psalm 119:103 How sweet are thy words unto my taste! yea, sweeter than honey to my mouth!

2 John
V.1-3
Key

An epistle is considered a formal letter. Most epistles begin with this salutation and in this same order.

John the disciple

V.1 The *elder*

V.1 unto the *elect lady* and her *children*

whom I love in the truth; and not I only, but also all they that have known the truth;

John was with Jesus and had known Him from the beginning of His Ministry on earth.

Immediately after the resurrection, Jesus appeared to the disciples and called them children because they were just beginning their own ministry. Now John considers himself an elder.

V.2 For the *truth's sake*, which dwelleth in us, and shall be with us for ever.

Jesus said I am the truth,...

G-R-A-C-E

God's riches at Christ's expense.

V.3 *Grace* be with you, *mercy*, and *peace*,

Grace is receiving blessings that we do not deserve. Mercy is not receiving punishments we do deserve.

from *God the Father*, and from the *Lord Jesus Christ*, the Son of the Father, in truth and love

2 John
V.1-3

John the disciple

V.1 The e_____

V.1 unto the e_____ l_____ and her c_____

whom I love in the truth; and not I only, but also all they that have known the truth;

John 2:14 I have written unto you, fathers, because ye have known him that is from the beginning.

V.2 For the t_____ s_____, which dwelleth in us, and shall be with us for ever.

.

V.3 G_____ be with you, m_____, and p_____,

from G_____ the F_____, and from the L_____ J_____ C_____, the Son of the Father, in truth and love

V.4 I rejoiced greatly that I found of thy *children walking in truth*, as we have received a commandment from the Father.

V.5 And now I beseech thee, lady, not as though I wrote a new commandment unto thee, but that which *we had from the beginning, that we love one another.*

V.6 *And this is love, that we walk after his commandments.* This is the commandment, That, as ye have heard from the beginning, ye should walk in it.

John 5:3 For this is the love of God, that we keep his commandments: and his commandments are not grievous.

2 John
V. 4-6

V.4 I rejoiced greatly that I found of thy c_____ w_____ in t_____, as we have received a commandment from the Father.

V.5 And now I beseech thee, lady, not as though I wrote a new commandment unto thee, but that which w_____ h_____ f_____ the b_____, that w____ l_____ o_____ a_____.

V.6 And this is l_____, that w_____ w_____ a_____ h____ c_____. This is the commandment, That, as ye have heard from the beginning, ye should walk in it.

John 5:3 For this is the love of God, that we keep his commandments: and his commandments are not grievous.

2 John V. 7-8 Key

V.7 For many *deceivers* are entered into the world, who *confess not* that Jesus Christ is come in the flesh. This is a deceiver and an *antichrist*.

1 John 4:2-3 Try the spirits

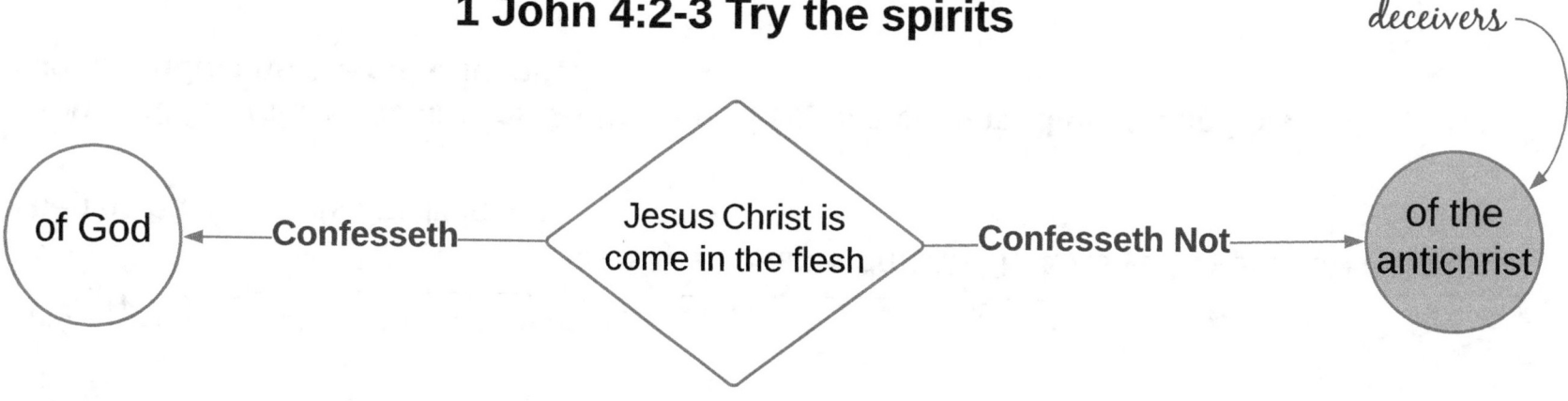

deceivers

of God ← **Confesseth** — Jesus Christ is come in the flesh — **Confesseth Not** → of the antichrist

False prophets come to steal and destroy the flock.

V.8 Look to yourselves, that we *lose* not those things which we have wrought, but that we receive a *full reward.*

Fellowship with the Father and the Son. Not just salvation.

dwell

John 2:24 Let that therefore abide in you, which ye have heard from the beginning. <u>If that which ye have heard from the beginning shall remain in you, ye also shall continue in the Son, and in the Father.</u>

fellowship

2 John V. 7-8

V.7 For many d_____ are entered into the world, who c_____ n_____ that Jesus Christ is come in the flesh. This is a deceiver and an a_____.

1 John 4:2-3 Try the spirits

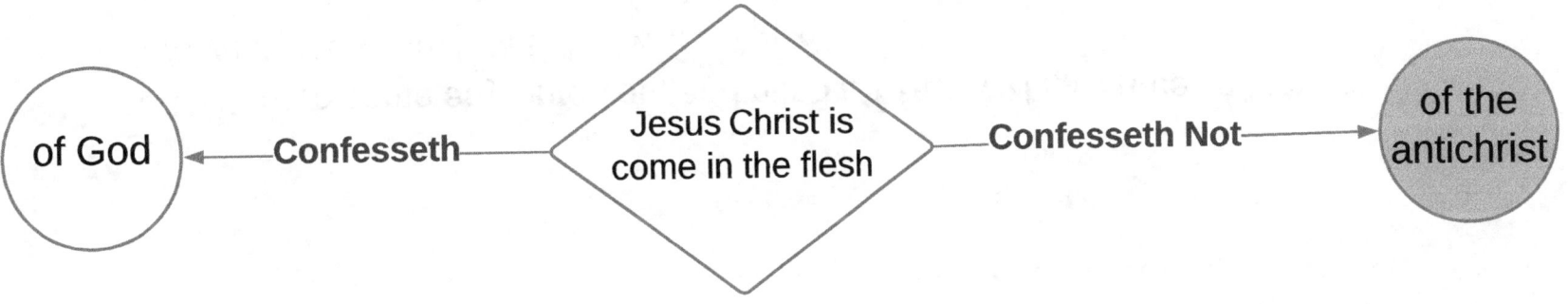

of God ←—Confesseth—— **Jesus Christ is come in the flesh** ——Confesseth Not——→ of the antichrist

V.8 Look to yourselves, that we l_____ not those things which we have wrought, but that we receive a f_____ r_____.

John 2:24 Let that therefore abide in you, which ye have heard from the beginning. If that which ye have heard from the beginning shall remain in you, ye also shall continue in the Son, and in the Father.

Jesus Christ is come in the flesh

V.9 Whosoever transgresseth, and abideth not in the doctrine of Christ, hath not God. He that *abideth* in the *doctrine of Christ, he hath both the Father and the Son.*

Religions that accept God but deny that Jesus is the Son of God, that has come in the flesh is antichrist.
You cannot have one without the other.

V.10 If there come any unto you, and bring *not this doctrine,* receive him not into your house, *neither bid him God speed:*

V. 11 For he that *biddeth him God speed is partaker of his evil deeds.*

Cults that knock on your door, who claim that Jesus is merely a created being, are not to be invited into your home. When trying the spirit, they have the spirit of antichrist and you become partaker in spreading doctrine against Jesus Christ.

2 John
V. 9-11

V.9 Whosoever transgresseth, and abideth not in the doctrine of Christ, hath not God. He that a_____ in the d_____ of C_____, he h_____ b_____ the F_____ and the S_____.

V.10 If there come any unto you, and bring n_____ this d_____, receive him not into your house, n_____ b_____ h_____ g_____ s_____:

V. 11 For he that b_____ h_____ g_____ s_____ is p_____ of h_____ e_____ d_____.

V.12 Having many things to write unto you, I would not write with *paper and ink*: but I trust to come unto you, and speak face to face, *that our joy may be full.*

3John 1:4 I have no greater joy than to hear that my children walk in truth.

V.13 The children of thy *elect sister* greet thee. *Amen.*

another church in the faith

Be it established

2 John
V. 12-13

V.12 Having many things to write unto you, I would not write with
p_____ and i_____: but I trust to come unto you, and speak face to
face, t_____ o_____ j_____ m_____ b___ f_____.

3John 1:4 I have no greater joy than to hear that my children walk in truth.

V.13 The children of thy e_____ s_____ greet thee. A_____.

Read III John

John 2:5 But whoso keepeth his word, in him verily is the love of God perfected: hereby know we that we are in him.

3 John
V.1-6
Key

John the disciple

V.1 The *elder*

V. 1 *wellbeloved Gaius*, whom I love in the truth.

V.2 Beloved, I wish above all things that thou mayest *prosper and be in health*, even as thy *soul prospereth*.

not just spiritually but physically also.

V.3 For I rejoiced greatly, when the brethren came and testified of the truth that is in thee, even as *thou walkest in the truth*.

Gaius

Gaius was a convert of John

V.4 I have *no greater joy than to hear that my children walk in truth*.

Gaius

V.5 Beloved, thou doest faithfully whatsoever thou doest to the brethren, and to strangers;

V.6 Which have borne witness *of thy charity before the church*: whom if thou bring forward on their journey after a godly sort, thou shalt do well:

brethern

Jesus

God is able to take care of His own

V.7 Because that for *his name's sake* they went forth, taking nothing of the Gentiles.

V. 8 We therefore ought to receive such, that we might be *fellowhelpers* to the truth.

God uses the church to help those in the ministry

3 John
V.1-6

John

V.1 The *elder*

V. 1 *wellbeloved Gaius*, whom I love in the truth.

V.2 Beloved, I wish above all things that thou mayest p_____ *and be in* h_____, even as thy s_____ p_____.

V.3 For I rejoiced greatly, when the brethren came and testified of the truth that is in thee, even as t_____ w_____ *in the* t_____.

V.4 I have n____ g_____ j____ t_____ *to* h_____ *that* m____ c_____ w_____ *in* t_____.

V.5 Beloved, thou doest faithfully whatsoever thou doest to the brethren, and to strangers;

V.6 Which have borne witness *of thy* c_____ *before the* c_____: whom if thou bring forward on their journey after a godly sort, thou shalt do well:

V.7 Because that for *his* n_____ s_____ they went forth, taking nothing of the Gentiles.

V. 8 We therefore ought to receive such, that we might be f_____ to the truth.

3 John
V.9-14
Key

John, the elder praised Gaius publicly for his good works. He advised the church of both types of members those that were evil and also those that were good.

the well beloved Gaius

Diotrephes

Church

Demetrius

John

assert leadership

Diotrephes

V.9 I wrote unto the church: but Diotrephes, who loveth to have the preeminence among them, receiveth us not.

V.10 Wherefore, if I come, I will remember his deeds which he doeth, prating against us with malicious words: and not content therewith, neither doth he himself receive the brethren, and forbiddeth them that would, and casteth them out of the church.

V.11 Beloved, follow not that which is evil, but that which is good. He that doeth good is of God: but he that doeth evil hath not seen God.

Demetrius

V.12 Demetrius hath good report of all men, and of the truth itself: yea, and we also bear record; and ye know that our record is true.

3 John
V.9-14

the wellbeloved
Gaius

Diotrephes

Demetrius

Church

John

V.9 I w_____ unto the c_____: but D_____, who loveth to have the p_____ among them, receiveth us not.

Diotrephes

V.10 Wherefore, if I come, I will remember his deeds which he doeth, p_____ against us with m_____ w_____: and not content therewith, neither doth he himself r_____ the b_____, and f_____ them that would, and c_____ them o_____ of the c_____.

V.11 Beloved, follow not that which is evil, but that which is good. He that doeth good is of God: but he that doeth evil hath not seen God.

Demetrius

V.12 D_____ hath g_____ r_____ of all men, and of the truth itself: yea, and we also bear record; and ye know that our record is true.

| 3 John
V.13-14
Key |
| --- |

John

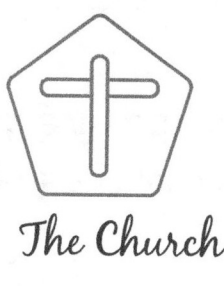

The Church

V.13 I had many things to write, but I will not with *ink and pen* write unto thee:

V.14 But I trust I shall shortly see thee, and we shall speak face to face. Peace be to thee. *Our friends salute thee. Greet the friends by name.*

3 John
V.13-14

John

The Church

V.13 I had many things to write, but I will not with i_____ and p_____ write unto thee:

V.14 But I trust I shall shortly see thee, and we shall speak face to face. Peace be to thee. O_____ f_____ s_____ thee. G_____ the f_____ by n_____.

To order additional titles or join our email list visit

www.CommonPeopleSeries.com

Titles currently available in the
Common People Series

The Book of Ruth
The Gospel According to John
The Epistles of I,II, III John
The Book of I Kings
The Epistle to the Romans

Contact us at
commonpeopleseries@gmail.com

www.ingramcontent.com/pod-product-compliance
Lightning Source LLC
Chambersburg PA
CBHW080846120626
46553CB00009B/2592